Experience
of a
Lifetime

Experience of a Lifetime

Stories
of
Life's Trials
and
Triumphs

ALMA HEATON

Published and Distributed by:

Cedar Fort, Incorporated
925 North Main, Springville, Ut 84663   801-489-4084

Cover Design by Lyle Mortimer
Page Layout and Design by Stephen J. Bons
Printed in the United States of America

ABOUT THE AUTHOR

The first twenty-eight years of Alma Heaton's life were spent in Kanab, Utah. At age 19 he went on a mission to Eastern Canada. He left the mission four months early because his father was dying of cancer.

He farmed, hearded sheep and cattle, ran a sawmill and was a trucker until he was 28 years old. At this time he joined the army, and was married to Marie Bishop on his first furlough home. Mr. Heaton spent 39 months in the army and was discharged at the Tooele Ordinance Depot in Tooele, Utah.

He went to Weber College in Ogden, Utah, and after graduation attended Utah State University in Logan, Utah, receiving a Master's Degree in Recreation and Physical Education. After graduation he taught the sixth grade in North Ogden for one year and in South Ogden for one year.

In 1953 he came to Brigham Young University to be in charge of recreation at the school.

He was a member of the M.I.A. General Board for fifteen years, was Chairman of the American Association of Health, Physical Education and Recreation, dance section, for one year. He would like to spend the rest of his life teaching social recreation for the Church.

ACKNOWLEDGMENT

This book is the result of an assignment I gave one of my classes: to write up the experience that taught them the greatest lesson. Twenty-five years later I have time to assemble them in book form.

I want to thank my family recreation class for the lesson these experiences have taught me, as well as those who will take time to read The Experiences of a Lifetime.

Reading over these experiences has given me a broader view of the purpose of life. I want to thank all the students that happened to be in my class at that time.

I want to acknowledge the invaluable assistance rendered by Professor Don Norton, Claire Foley, and his class for editing these experiences and following through with details.

I was so carried away with these experiences when I first read them that I filed them away, hoping that sometime before I passed to the other side, I would have time to put them in a book so others could learn from them and write episodes from their own life history.

I give credit to the students for turning in an outstanding assignment. A few words may have been changed, but the thoughts are theirs. Since words do not always give the same meaning to every person who reads them, they can at least inspire meaning to those who have had similar experiences.

PREFACE

Experiences—good and bad—make up the fabric of our lives. The intelligent person learns to avoid the bad experiences and repeat the good ones, shaping habits and attitudes for a happy and productive life.

Our own experiences are the best teachers, but certainly not the only ones. The purpose of this book is to show that the experiences of others can be important in shaping our lives. Benjamin Franklin put it another way in his Poor Richard's Almanac when he wrote: "Experience keeps a dear school, but fools will learn in no other."

None of us has enough time to live through the experiences necessary to learn how to cope with life. We must lean on what others have discovered through trial and error. When Patrick Henry, speaking in the Virginia Convention in 1775, said, "I have but one lamp by which my feet are guided and that is the lamp of experience," he spoke of the experiences of others as well as his own. He added, "I know of no way of judging the future but by the past."

People of all ages can use these stories as background in Family Home Evening activities, religion classes, church talks, and other settings. Each of the happenings is summed up in a lesson application which can be of vicarious value to all.

"For all experience," said Henry Brooks Adams, "is an arch, to build upon."

WHY WRITE PERSONAL EXPERIENCES

Many church leaders have written their personal experiences—not that great individuals keep records, but people who write experiences may become great.

The Prophet Joseph Smith counseled the Saints to keep records as well as lessons learned through their experiences. The use people make of their experiences (good or bad) is very important.

If a person can laugh at himself as he makes mistakes, he is likely to keep a healthy mind as well as body.

Elder Paul Dunn, commenting on this point, once said, "Tragedy plus time equals humor."

I urge you to carry a notebook with you at all times and start jotting down your experiences as you recall them. Write down lessons you learned about yourself, about others, and about the Church.

If we do not write down our experiences we will forget them and may have to learn them over again.

After we have had an experience, we should take time to digest the meaning, which may be usable to all others.

I promise you that you cannot fail in this project and that you will bless your family for generations to come.

> You
> You are the fellow who has to decide
> Whether you'll do it or toss it aside.
> You are the fellow who makes up your mind
> Whether you'll lead or linger behind.
> Whether you'll try for the goal that's far,
> Or just be contented to stay where you are.
> Take it or leave it, here's something to do!
> Just think it over—It's all up to you.
>
> —J. Edgar Guest

TABLE OF CONTENTS

FAITH

DAD'S HAND

As a young girl, I went to my grandfather's farm, which is two miles north of Manti, Utah. Dad and I were walking, hand in hand, over some big rocks by the corral. I told my father that I didn't need to hold his hand any more, so I let go. After walking a short distance, I fell on the rocks. I received a big cut—for a four-year-old—on my forehead. I now have a small scar to remind me of the important lesson I learned that day—that I do need the help and guidance of parents who are wiser than me.

APPRECIATING SIMPLE THINGS

Walk here and there, stand up and sit down, bend over, and climb stairs. I do these things daily, but didn't ever give them a second thought until about two years ago. I had been doing too many things and was overdoing it. My poor body was ready to give out on me, but I kept going, kept playing on the basketball team. Then my left knee began to give me great pain. One night, I couldn't even stand up. I cried because it hurt so badly.

I was taken to the hospital that night and given some pain medication. I was told to rest awhile, and then to use crutches when I went back to school. I did this, but still was in much pain. In fact, it became just as painful in my right knee. It was so bad that I couldn't even put a sheet over my knees at night because my knees were so swollen and sore. I would come home at night and cry because of the pain, of which I told very few people.

The pain actually lessened for a time, and I just kept going. However, I finally had to work with a specialist, who gave me shots and medication and charged me to rest, to quit playing sports and to stop mountain climbing—to stop all the things I loved to do. For two months, I had large casts on both legs. It was an awful time, and I hated it. They were so heavy that I couldn't do anything, not even rest because it was so awkward. I just couldn't wait until I could run again, could feel free to go anywhere. I couldn't even kneel down to say my prayers. And the casts hardly relieved the pain, so I had to have surgery. (Only on one leg at a time, though— thank goodness.)

The surgery was the most painful thing. I stayed in bed for awhile but recovered quickly because of my willingness to do special therapy—in spite of the pain. Pain is an awful thing. No one liked to be with me because I felt so mean and irritable. I had forgotten what happiness and joy were like. I don't understand how my family put up with all of this.

I was determined to walk again, so I kept working with the therapy. After the surgery and my recovery, I felt less pain. It was such a relief when I could walk again, even with crutch- es—to go outside, to see people and even to hear the birds sing. I had been inside for so long that I was more grateful for the small things, like sunshine, rain, trees, and grass. I felt joyful over this new beauty that had always been there with- out my taking the time to look at it. Soon I even began to run. The happiness I felt at being able to enjoy God's beauty can't be described.

I now feel much more empathy for those who are sick or in the hospital. I will never forget the many sleepless nights and the times that I cried out in pain. I will never forget how I wished to go outside and do things as other people did, to go to school. I wanted to have relief from all that pain even for one hour. But I learned some very special things from this experience.

I learned to love and appreciate the small, simple things that are around me daily. I have a deeper love for the nature around me and for my friends and family. I am more sensitive to other people and try harder to help others. I try to be more understanding of those who are in pain, knowing how difficult it is at times to smile. I learned a new thankfulness now that my body is well—I can walk and see and hear the things of beauty around me. I am also so thankful to be able to kneel down at night by my bed and pour out my heart with thanks unto my Father in Heaven. I also learned of the great power of the priesthood, for I was blessed many times and felt of its presence and power. I am thankful for this experience and what I have learned from it. It has been a true blessing to me.

HEAVENLY HELP

I grew up on a ranch in Arizona. My dad always made us work very hard, and we learned to love it. We are a close family, and we always play and work together.

One Christmas we were bringing our cattle home from the mountain pastures for the winter. It was a cold, windy day, and the cattle had been moving slowly all day long. It was getting close to dark, and my dad didn't think we would make it to the corral before dark, so he sent me into town to get the horse trailer. As I was coming back, about five miles from the herd I started to have problems. The road was hilly and had lots of cinders on it.

As I went up one of the hills, I came down the other side and there was a sharp curve in the road. I tried to turn, but the pickup and gooseneck trailer slid about eight feet off the road. I immediately shifted the gear to reverse and tried to back up, but my wheels started spinning and the truck began to sink further into the cinders. Being the controlled person that I am, I started to cry; but then I got out of the pickup to look over the situation.

There was a big rock in front of my right tire, so I didn't see any way that I could go forward. I had already tried backing out with no result, so I was beginning to get desperate. I even began walking toward the herd, but decided that I wouldn't get far before it would become completely dark. Then I sat down on a rock and began to pray.

Suddenly a very calm feeling came over me, and I got back into the pickup. I shifted into first gear and slowly drove forward and back onto the road. I made it back to the herd within a few minutes, and I was never happier to see a bunch of old dumb cows than I was at that time.

I learned the powerful influence of prayer. Before I said my prayer, I was almost hysterical and could not think properly. But when I said the prayer, I became very calm and knew that my Heavenly Father would help me.

A Drive Up the Canyon

I went home one weekend to see my family and friends, and to get a little rest and relaxation. Friday night had been a little dull because nobody was home and there was nothing to do. I was bored. I was afraid Saturday would be the same.

Saturday afternoon I got a telephone call from one of my friends. She wanted to go for a ride because she felt the same way I did. We didn't know where to go, so we decided to drive up the canyon. I asked my mom if I could take a drive up the canyon with our car. She advised me not to go because the roads were icy, and if I got stuck there would be no one to help me out. Also, two girls in the canyon alone isn't the greatest idea. Someone might try to run us off the road.

Wanting to do something all day, I told her we would go up just a little ways and that I'd be careful, and if it got bad I'd turn around and come back. I made it sound like she could trust me. Besides, I hadn't done a thing all day.

So I picked up my friend and proceeded to go up the canyon. Upon entering we noticed that a lot of people of not a high caliber were also going up the canyon. Very shortly we found out why.   They were having what is called a "beer bust."

Looking behind us, I noticed we were being followed by four boys in a car. The roads were getting very icy to where it was hard to keep the car on the road. I couldn't stop because if I did stop, the boys in the car would stop also. I could see we were approaching a hill, and I knew we wouldn't be able to make it to the top. As I pulled to the side the boys passed me, and went up the canyon, but who knew for how long?

As I started to back out, my car started sliding. I panicked, hit the brakes and slid off the side of the road. I wished right then that I had listened to my mom! She was always right. All I could see was Mom telling me that she had advised me not to go, and now look at the mess I was in. Then another worry came to my mind. What would happen if those boys returned?

Trying very hard now to get the car onto the road, I found I couldn't. The harder I tried, the more the car slipped closer to the trees—plus the car started sinking deeper into the snow. I must admit I was scared more then than I had ever been in my life—I was all alone. What was I to do? I remembered a story I had heard about something like this, and what helped the people was to pray to Father in Heaven. That was it—we'd pray also. I would pray first and my friend would pray second. I don't know how she felt. She must have been embarrassed because she said, "No, I'll let you pray, OK?"

I knew then that I would have to have power and faith for both of us. I knew we would get out safely and that the car would be unharmed. Upon closing, I looked at my friend and told her that we'd get out unharmed. She had a look in her eye that let me know she believed it, too.

She got out to guide the car back down. I started the car up, turned the wheels and backed out without even as much as a little slide. I'll never forget the feeling I had. I just had to thank Heavenly Father for helping me.

Turning around with no problem, we arrived safely home. We never saw those boys again, and our testimonies that God lives and loves his children were strengthened. A testimony of the power of prayer was also in our hearts. I know that God lives and that he answers prayers if we pray with faith and real intent.

FAITH TO BE HEALED

Several weeks ago, I was having quite a few problems with school. I decided that I would not burden others with these problems, and so I didn't tell anyone about my difficulties. I did spend some time discussing them with the Lord, but somehow, it was not the outlet I needed. I didn't realized this until all of my anxieties began to take a toll on my physical well-being. One night, I got a rash all over my body. Even worse, my feet became partially paralyzed and I could not walk for twenty-four hours.

It was so painful to take a step that I finally decided to stop trying, and I began crawling around the house to get where I needed to go. This made me worry all the more, and not knowing if my condition was permanent added even more stress to my list of worries.

My father and brother saw my frustration and gave me a special priesthood blessing in which they told me that my burdens would be lifted. They advised me to seek for peace and not worry about those things that I could not control at that time. They also gave me a blessing of health that I might be able to walk again as usual and return to my school and work duties. The morning after my blessing, I could walk without pain, and I no longer felt the weight of my burdens. I was filled with gratitude toward the Lord because he had healed both my physical and emotional afflictions. I was thankful that my father and brother were worthy to give me a priesthood blessing, but most of all, I was thankful for the lesson of faith that had been taught to me. I had faith that I would be well in the morning, and I was.

PRIESTHOOD MIRACLE

One morning, my mom was curling her hair with a curling iron when it slipped. The end of the iron poked her in the eye and burned her cornea. The doctor told her that the cornea was damaged severely and she would need a transplant before she'd be able to see again. He gave her some cortisone drops to minimize the pain, and gave her instructions to put them in her eye every two hours. When Mom returned home, she immediately asked for a priesthood blessing from two men in our ward.

At the time of Mom's accident, my younger sister had been laid up because of her recent back surgery, and Mom knew that she needed to regain her sight if she was going to take care of my sister.

Through the power of the priesthood and Mom's faith, she never needed the cornea transplant. The doctor couldn't believe it. He couldn't understand how the cortisone could have healed a damaged cornea. But we knew it was a miracle and that the priesthood, not the cortisone, had saved her sight.

HAVING FAITH

When I was fourteen-years-old, I contracted the mumps. These eventually turned into a more serious disease called spinal meningitis. I was so sick that I had to be admitted to the county hospital. The illness causes a person to go into convulsions and shake all over, so I had to have a private room in the hospital. While I was in one of the convulsions, my dad and a friend came into my room and gave me a blessing. Immediately my shaking quit and I felt completely well. Because of my recovery, I learned how important it is to have faith in the healing power of the priesthood.

TRUST

It was the summertime and my family was traveling to Utah from New Jersey. Late one night we were in Cheyenne, Wyoming. My mother was driving and everyone else was asleep. The road was straight and stretched out for miles. Pretty soon, my mother fell asleep and ran off the road down a steep embankment. Fortunately, we rode down the embankment and did not roll over because our load was very heavy.

By the time we reached the bottom, my father was awake and so was my mother but she wasn't sure what had happened. The problem we now had was how to get out of the gully we were in. It was too steep to drive back up the embankment. Just then, a motorist who had seen us go down looked over the top of the embankment, yelling down to see if everything was okay. My father told him everything was fine, but that we had no way of getting back on the road. The motorist then told us that if we followed the gully for a while, it would soon level off and meet with the road.

We followed his instructions. Soon the road did level with the ground and we were able to get back on the road and on our way again. By trusting his advice, we were able to recover and continue on our way.

WORTHY OFFERINGS

I had been paying six percent of my babysitting money toward the church building fund, along with my regular tithing. I knew that I needed a summer job, and I wanted to be worthy to ask Heavenly Father for help. Two days before school let out, I applied for a job. The employer had already filled the position I had applied for, but had a better position available and I got that job. I knew then that Heavenly Father had blessed me because I had been paying my tithing and helping to fund the building of a chapel.

THE BLESSINGS OF TITHING

When my older brother Ronald turned nineteen, he decided to go on a mission. He hadn't saved very much money or prepared himself in all the areas he could have, but he was determined to serve a mission. After he made his decision, he started to prepare himself and save money. Unfortunately, my brother liked to spend money. He had a yellow Volkswagen bug that he loved to work on and improve with all of the latest gadgets. He was planning on selling his car for a large amount of money and then using that money to fund his mission.

Ronald tried for a long time to sell his car. He put a sign in the window and ads in the newspaper, but no one wanted to buy his car. Then, while getting everything finalized for his mission, it was discovered that Ronald hadn't paid his tithing for a long time. My mother and father told him that he wouldn't sell his car until the tithing had been paid. So Ronald began to catch up on his tithing, but still no one showed interest in buying his car. Four days before he was to leave on his mission, he finished paying all of his tithing. The next day, he sold his car. The Lord does bless us when we pay our tithing.

ONE HEADLIGHT

Late one night after work, I learned the importance of listening to and following the promptings of the Spirit. I had been working as a short-order cook late into the night and was very tired as I got in my car to drive home. The night was very dark; there was no moon, and the clouds covered any starlight. My eyes drooped as I drove home.

Far up the road I saw a motorcycle coming toward me. As I looked at the motorcycle's headlight, I thought about how lonely it must be to be out alone on a motorcycle on this black night. Then something told me to move over on the road far to the right side. At first I thought, "How silly. How much room does one motorcycle need on the road?" But the feeling came back stronger that I should move over and give the oncomer all the room I could.

As I pulled over just in time to let him pass, I realized that it was actually a car with a missing headlight, and it was straddling the middle line. Had I not moved over we would have surely crashed.

LISTENING TO THE SPIRIT

While my husband Bob and I were dating, we had a very frightening experience in December of 1969, in Hawaii. There was a big storm in Alaska that had been causing very high waves on the north shore of Oahu. Bob and I decided to watch these giant waves for a while near Sunset Beach. We were watching the waves from a high embankment and felt safe, except that we both had a strong feeling that we should leave. We didn't pay attention to this spiritual warning and shortly after, a sixty foot wave came in and hit the embankment where we were standing. We tried to run, but were too slow. The water hit the embankment and shot up. Tons of water crashed down on top of us and smashed us into the road. We were very blessed to walk away with only broken bones and a concussion. Others on the island had been drowned or washed out to sea by that wave. I spent a month in the hospital and another month in painful physical therapy because I hadn't listened to the Spirit's warning.

THE SPIRIT'S WHISPERS

My family were returning home from summer vacation and we were fairly close to home. My father wanted to drive through the night and reach home before morning. We were all tired and really didn't care what he did; if my dad was willing to drive that long, we weren't going to complain—anyway, we could sleep in the car. A few minutes after the decision was made, my mother insisted for some strange reason to stop where we were at and spend the night in our trailer. She was so persistent on stopping that my father heeded her request. We spent the night in our trailer, and when morning came we continued our journey home. A few miles ahead of the place we had camped, we discovered an awful avalanche that had occurred during the night at approximately the same time we would have been traveling through that canyon. If it had not been for my mother's strange prompting to stop, we might have been caught in that avalanche.

FEEDING THE FIVE THOUSAND OR THE SEVEN?

When my parents were younger, the missionaries stopped by unexpectedly just as my mom was making up some lunch. She didn't know what to do because she barely had enough to feed our family of five. But just the same, she invited them to say and have a bite to eat. Surprisingly enough (or perhaps not) the food never ran out. There was enough for all. After the missionaries had left she looked in the bowl and there was still some tuna left.

This experience has taught me the importance of keeping the commandments so that the Lord can be with you in times of need. When we are generous and give, the Lord will provide for us. This experience has also taught me to believe the bible story of feeding the five thousand. The Lord can work such miracles.

THREE LOST BOYS

Several years ago we had a family reunion at Yellowstone National Park, and we camped at the Old Faithful Campground. We had just finished putting away the breakfast dishes when we noticed that the three oldest boys had disappeared. Two of them were my brothers and the other was my cousin. My other cousin and I headed over to the nearby lake that the boys had frequented, but returned with the report that they were not there. Quickly our family hopped into the car and drove around the campground.

After about an hour of driving there was still no sign of them. We checked the lake again and then went to the ranger station to involve the rangers in the search. With renewed efforts we set out again, but we had a family prayer first. By this time the boys had been missing for three or four hours. We were almost frantic. For another hour we searched with the rangers, who used their loudspeakers to try and find them.

Finally, the rangers sent us back to our campsite to wait while they finished the search. Once again we knelt in prayer to our Father in Heaven that somewhere our boys were safe and on their way back. We arose from our knees and went about preparing the next meal rather half-heartedly. As my cousin and I went over to get water, we spotted also off in the distance three very tired, sore-footed boys. We ran over to them, knowing that the Lord had answered our prayers.

A COMFORTING ANSWER TO PRAYER

I am a lover of cats, especially Siamese cats, and I have owned and raised many of them. The first time I received an answer to a prayer was when one of my Siamese cats, Rex, was very sick and near death. I had been home all afternoon, feeding Rex with an eye dropper because he was too sick to eat. To see one of my cats in such agony and pain just tore my heart out. I love them almost as much as I love my family.

It was about two o'clock in the afternoon, and I had an orthodontist appointment at three o'clock. Before I left, I prayed that Father in Heaven would remove Rex's misery, either by making him well or by taking him home. For me to ask that one of my cats be taken home showed a great love for life.

I went to my appointment, and when I came home, I had a very peaceful feeling. I found out that my little brother was out burying Rex. This was the first time that I did not cry at the death of one of my babies, and I know that it was because my prayer was answered.

AFRAID OF THE DARK

When I was growing up I was, and still am, deathly afraid of the dark. I can't remember any specific experience that instilled this fear in me, but as far as I can remember I have always had it. I recall lying in bed at night, suffocating underneath the covers, afraid to even peek my head out. Since my bedroom was located downstairs, going to bed was an even more dramatic event for me. Each night I would put on my pajamas, and then in a single motion, turn off the light by the door and take a flying leap for the covers. Once inside the safety of the quilts I would close my eyes as tight as possible and pray with all the vigor a little child can and ask Heavenly Father to please not make it so dark in the room. Even as young as I was, it never ceased to amaze me how quickly he would answer my prayers. Each night as I opened my eyes, it would be just enough lighter that I could make out the familiar forms in my room. This helped to ease my fears, and I would soon fall asleep.

I never questioned my faith in the power of prayer until one day in a health class in the ninth grade. I learned that this had not been an answer to my prayer but simply the small circle in my eye growing larger to let in more light, thereby enabling me to see better.

For several years after that, my prayers were said just a little bit less sincerely, and I don't think I really expected an answer. I'll always be grateful to the Lord. I was reading my scriptures one morning and read the verse which states that God knows all things and knows all of our wants and needs. It hit me then how misled I had been. Long ago in the eternities God had realized that some little girl on his earth would be deathly afraid of the dark. So as a kind father would, he created us so magnificently that our eyes would function in this manner. If we could only hold on to that faith that we held as young children, our lives would be so much richer. We would be as his sheep that know the sound of the Master's voice and obey it. "My sheep hear my voice and I know them, and they follow me; And I give unto them Eternal life."

THE POWER OF ONE PRAYER

My girl friend and I went to a party out in the country on Halloween. After getting out of the car, we made sure to lock the doors only to discover the headlights were still on. The key only worked in one door, so we went to open it. But it wouldn't open. We tried the other door just to be sure and then went back and kept trying the door the key was supposed to work in. We had no luck. My friend's dad would be upset (to put it mildly) if we ended up with a dead battery. We went to a house where a grumbly old man said he would come out, but he couldn't open the door either. He went back to the house for something and I suggested that we pray while he was gone. Afterwards I said, "Okay Gen, one more time and it'll work," and it did. After fifty tries one prayer opened the door.

The Lost Ring

One night I went with my family to see a play at the high school. We went with a man and his wife who were friends of our family's, and as it turned out, their seats were directly in front of ours. I'm sure that we all enjoyed the play, although I no longer remember what it was about. What I do remember is that during the performance, I was absently twisting and pulling at a ring I was wearing. It was not a very valuable ring, but it had belonged to my mother when she was a young girl, and she had recently given it to me. As I was pulling at it, it came off and slipped out of my fingers. I tried to look for it on the floor around my feet, but the auditorium was dark, and I couldn't find it. After the play was over and the lights were on, we all searched for the ring, looking up and down the aisles surrounding our seats. Although we searched until everyone else had left the auditorium, we could not find it. By this time I was so upset that I started to cry. There was nothing left to do but go home. My parents said that we could call the school the next day and perhaps a janitor would have found it.

I went home and got in bed, still silently praying, as I had been earlier, that somehow I would find my ring. A few minutes later the phone rang. It was the man we had been with that night, and he had my ring. It seems that the ring had somehow fallen straight into his back pocket. As I think of it now, it still seems almost a miracle that this could have happened, especially since his seat had not even been directly in front of mine. However it happened, my prayer was answered, and in such a dramatic way. I thanked our Father in heaven and have not forgotten what he did.

Against the Odds

When I was two and a half years old I got spinal meningitis and was put into the hospital where about ten other chil-

dren had the same disease. I was unable to eat, was fed intra-
venously, and was given eighty penicillin shots. The doctors
gave my parents little hope that I would live. They fasted
and prayed with family members and friends, and at the end
of the fast they met in a prayer circle. The man praying said
that I would live, and the Spirit bore witness to the others
that this was true. I did live and didn't have any physical
handicaps. Sadly, however, all the other children died. I
learned from this experience that the Lord has the power to
save and bring to pass miracles. These miracles are a result
of the faith and prayers of the righteous.

THE LOST TWENTY DOLLARS

Not too long ago I was a member of the Morgan High
School drill team. We were preparing for a trip to compete
in the Calgary, Canada parade, so every Saturday morning at
six o'clock we were up and practicing. We marched around
the football field and around the not-very-large city of
Morgan. The band was right there with us, and it seemed it
played louder in the early morning than at any other time. I
always wondered if it was because the band members knew
their parents were still in bed.

One morning I remember how happy I was to be able to
pay the last twenty dollars of my bus fare for the Canada trip.
I had the money in my Levi pocket and was going to pay as
soon as I got to practice. I didn't have a chance to pay the
band director and completely forgot about the money until I
got home. Mom asked me if I felt good that the last of the
money was paid. I felt in my Levi pocket. The money was
gone. Twenty dollars may not seem like a lot, but when it is
hard earned money that is the means for going on a trip, it is
an awfully lot.

Mom told me to get in the car, and we drove around the
football field and the streets where we marched. I remember

I was sure there was no way I would ever see a green twenty dollar bill on a green football field or in the grass of a front lawn. We had looked about a half hour on the football field when I decided that the search was useless without Heavenly Father. I said a silent prayer and I asked for his guidance. We started driving home when I asked Mom to stop. I walked to the side of the road, and there caught under a sprinkler head was my twenty dollar bill. I know that there is no way on earth I would have found that money without Heavenly Father's help.

GOD'S PROTECTION

About three years ago, my sister, her boyfriend, and I were traveling from Twin Falls, Idaho to Provo, Utah. Before we left, I suggested that we have a prayer. We hadn't been gone long when a tire blew out. My sister was driving the Volkswagen, and she lost control. We swerved from one side of the highway to the other, went off the highway, and turned over three times.

It was a most frightening experience. It totaled the car, but we all walked away without any serious injuries. No one could believe we were not killed. We were grateful for God's protection that day.

A THANKSGIVING MIRACLE

It was on Thanksgiving day at the Fort Berthold Reservation when I discovered prayer to be the key to everything in the world. My companion and I were on our way to a member's home for a Thanksgiving dinner. We were early, so we decided to investigate a family's house which was secluded. There was a lot of snow on the ground, and it was very cold. The house was down in a gully, so to speak, and the road that led to the house was covered with snow and ice. Without thinking, I drove down the hill to the house. No one was home, so we decided to go back before we missed our dinner. Then we started up the hill. The truck almost made it to the top, but then started to swerve. The tires dug in the snow and we weren't going anywhere. I attempted several times to free the tires, yet was unsuccessful. I was very frustrated and scared. The thought to pray entered my mind, but I was too frustrated to want to pray. However, my wonderful companion suggested a prayer. I didn't feel like praying, so he prayed to help us get up the hill. After the prayer, I tried moving the truck again and was still not successful. We backed up to examine the situation and realized we didn't have any weight in the back of the truck for traction. We looked around and found some stones in a pile and began to load the pickup with the stones. After loading the truck, my companion, as skinny as he was, got in the back for added weight. We began moving up the hill and made it to the top. Both of us gave out a loud yell of success. We also made it on time for our appointment and had a wonderful dinner. During our visit, I wondered if we had got out of our predicament by coincidence or luck.

After dinner, we left the house and discovered that the temperature had dropped to about 30 degrees below zero. Had we not got up the hill, we would have frozen to death. Our pickup truck was low on gas, we didn't have sufficient clothing, especially on our feet, and the closest house next to the one we were stalled at was about five miles away. We would have never made it with only our oxford type shoes on.

This experience with prayer taught me that we should trust in the Lord in everything. If we live a righteous life and keep the commandments, the Lord will help us in times of need.

INDIVIDUAL WORTH

THE BLUE PACIFIER

"Today our English lesson is on page... Phyllis will you please take your thumb out of your mouth. You're not even paying attention!"

Her head lowered, she slowly wiped the fat thumb dry. Snickers and rude remarks were heard from the class. "If you keep sucking your that thing, one of these days it's going to fall off." Everyone laughed.

One day the teacher thought things had gone far enough. He and some of the boys in the class decided that if Phyllis got embarrassed to death, she would quit sucking her thumb.

It was just after lunch and class was about to begin. "Phyllis, would you come to the front of the room. It looks like we have a gift here for you."

Only a few kids knew about the gift, and when she opened it, she made no remarks, but just had a blank stare. "Well, what is it?" "Are you going to show us or not?" With no expression on her face, she pulled out a blue pacifier.

Trying her hardest to withstand the pressure, she quickly put it back in the box and started for her seat. Kids were laughing and mocking her. I watched her, blinded by tears, take her seat.

How can anyone honestly think that treating Phyllis as a baby or the odd one would help her problem? I could see how badly she was hurt, yet I sat there.

Phyllis left the room. If I had been her, I would have never come back. I didn't want anything to do with her, and neither did any of my friends. Why should I bother with her? I thought. I had everything I wanted. I had my friends. I got good grades and was popular.

But suddenly I found myself defending her. I had no control over my anger when I told them it was the cruelest thing anyone could have done. And then I sat down.

If you have done it unto the least of these, you have done it unto me.

CATHY

I have been teaching gymnastics every summer. Last summer, I had a girl in my class named Cathy. She was heavier than the rest and was a slow learner. She had a poor self-image. I noticed this and would talk to her often after class. I would always build her up. I spent extra time with her before and after class. She started to gain more confidence in herself and began to improve. She passed half the students in the class. And she was a much happier person because someone noticed her.

A little concern and awareness to help someone can change that person's life for the better.

LOVE CHANGES EVERYTHING

While attending Oregon State University, I participated in the Church Institute program. At the beginning of spring term, a girl by the name of Darlene started coming out to our meetings and activities. Darlene was 21 years old and was sloppy and backward in appearance.

Darlene had never finished high school and her mother had died when Darlene was quite young. She was then sent from relative to relative, never receiving the love and attention every child needs.

Several of the students decided they would help Darlene. Everyone tried to be friendly and warm towards her. She was eventually baptized and finished high school by passing the

G.E.D. test to obtain her diploma. All Darlene needed was to know that people cared for her and that she was needed.

Darlene was given a job as magazine representative, and she soon started taking better care of her grooming and clothes. When she came out of her shell we found that she was a very creative and clever girl who would do anything to help someone. Her testimony grew, and she had a very sweet spirit.

Without the help of the students, Darlene would have gone unnoticed. It was the special love and compassion given to her that helped her.

It makes me feel good to know that there are people who care and will go the extra mile to help their fellowmen. Darlene became a challenge and it was met with love. The gospel is love. We all need to share it with our fellowmen.

PIONEER TREK

My seminary class went on a pioneer trek in the desert last summer. We dressed like pioneers, complete with long dresses, suspenders, hats, and boots. There were about 150 students, and we had covered wagons and horses, to make it as authentic as possible. We started walking at 9:00 and walked until 5:00. It was about nine miles or so to the edge of the river. I learned what the pioneers must have gone through. My feet hurt after four hours. It's hard to imagine how it would hurt after several months.

We should never judge another until we have walked in their shoes. We can judge the future by the past—if we have the same experience and interpret the lesson in light of the gospel.

DEATH OF A CHILD

About three weeks ago my husband and I received a phone call from his home in Arizona. We learned that my husband's favorite niece had been hit and killed by a car. She was only six—and was the prettiest little girl I've ever seen. I realize that it is easy to say something like that about any cute little girl who has something like this happen to her, but she was very pretty. She was also very active and bright.

When we lived by the family in Arizona, she sometimes frightened me because she could sense my feelings and use them to her advantage. She must have liked me, because she always wanted to sit by me in church and Sunday School. I was constantly trying to avoid her, because she sometimes annoyed me.

We know she was taken for a purpose because of the circumstances of the accident and because of her dynamic personality. We knew she would could accomplish tremendous good in the spirit world.

I learned a personal lesson, but a lesson that I think most people can profit by. I really did care for my husband's niece; I thought about her often, thought about what I could do for her, but I didn't do anything. Since her death, I've wished many times that I could hug her and tell her thanks for being Laura. We need to let people know that we perceive their good qualities and appreciate them; we need to keep our thanks and our apologies up-to-date.

ALL HIS CHILDREN

When I went to California to live with my sister, I needed a job—one that would help me attain some goals I had set for myself. One such goal was to gain that inner peace of realizing that I am me—a child of God (no more and yet no less than anyone else), and also to be able to give of myself and learn charity. Besides this, I wanted to be home on the weekends and evenings to accomplish other important goals. So I discussed this with Heavenly Father in much prayer and fasting. I soon accepted a teaching job working with multi-handi-

capped children.   Over two hundred people were on the waiting list and many still applying at the time I was. But the Lord
wanted me to have this job and touched the hearts of those
hiring, for I was picked out of all of those to be the one to
have the interview. Soon after, I was accepted for the position.

I learned more about loving, giving and sharing than
any of my other experiences combined. Those children
gave me so much love, and all I could do was return it with
gratitude.   I learned to love them, accept myself, and be
receptive and giving to other's needs. Those precious little
children of Heavenly Father's, who, in spite of being crip-
pled, blind and deaf, and in spite of emotional problems,
had love in their hearts and were happy to be there. From
this miracle I gained a burning testimony of God's love for
all his children.

GETTING TO KNOW HEAVENLY FATHER

For about a month during my high school career, I
rebelled against my parents and friends. I lost my desire to
pray, and ultimately jeopardized my relationship with God
and the Church. This was the most miserable period of my
entire life. And yet the whole time this was happening, I kept
telling myself I didn't want to feel this way. I knew that if I
would start praying and asking for help, I could overcome
how I was feeling. But I just wasn't able to do it on my own.

In March of 1973, I went to Youth Conference. We spent
one day attending seminars and listening to three speakers
talk on different topics that are essential to our salvation.
One guest speaker really impressed me with his comments
and his ability to relate to us on an individual level. His name
was John Lund, and he spoke on developing a meaningful
relationship with God. He emphasized that we should read
the scriptures often, and pray daily.   He stressed that in our
prayers it is important that we get to know God personally.

He is our Father and our friend, and he is always there. We can learn to really know him.

When Brother Lund had finished his comments he looked at me, sitting in the middle of the audience, and asked my name. Then he said, "Lori, I want you to go home from this conference and start reading the scriptures and praying about them. And when you pray, get down on your knees and really pray to God so you can get to know Him." He gave me his address and asked my to write a letter to him to tell him how I had changed and how this affected my life. I was very overcome. Tears filled my eyes to think that Brother Lund had chosen me, out of our entire group, at the time in my life when I needed it most.

I went home from that Youth Conference feeling very inspired. I went to work reading the scriptures for thirty minutes every morning, and kneeling in prayer at least twice a day. Things happened slowly, but I could feel the changes in my life. I was happier, and I began getting along with my friends and family. I also found myself joining in more church and school activities. It was a wonderful feeling, and I knew that Lord was helping me in everything I did.

After a few months had passed, I wrote to Brother Lund and thanked him for giving me that challenge and related to him how much happier my life had become since I started reading the scriptures and praying. It's amazing what the Lord will do for you if you only ask. I truly believe he inspires his servants to say and do certain things for the benefit of those they come in contact with. Brother Lund reached my heart in an exciting way, and I'll always be thankful to him and to my Heavenly Father.

JUDGING OTHERS

I was at my grandma's house one day, and as I was talking to her, another girl from the neighborhood walked in. She

came right in the kitchen and started talking to my grand-
mother. I just sat there, watching this weird girl take the stage.
While she was talking, I picked her apart. I thought she was
ugly, weird, and had no manners. When she finally left, I told
Grandma what I had thought about this strange girl. But then
she told me that the girl was nineteen years old and mentally
retarded. The girl couldn't help the way she was.

KATHY

I met Kathy during my second semester of college. She
was to be my stand partner in the viola section of the
school orchestra for the entire semester. At first I thought it
would be fun to have an experienced college student for a
partner, but it seemed Kathy resented the fact that I was
her "superior" by one chair, and I resented the fact that I
was "always" wrong and she was "always" absolutely right—
even if she made the same mistakes I did. By the end of
about four weeks we were trying our best to ignore each
other, which is difficult when you share the same music.
Eight weeks into the semester we were not speaking to each
other at all.

I felt that Kathy was stuck up, snobbish and impossible,
and she probably felt the same or worse about me. I can see
now that we ruined an opportunity to learn because we were
too foolish to try and work out our differences. Had we
cooperated, we would have gained much more from orchestra that semester. As it was, we actually lost skill because of the
hostility between us.

Near the end of the semester I had a terrible day when
nothing had gone right. When Kathy appeared, I was sure
the worst part of the day had arrived. She asked me why I was
so gloomy, and we had a good talk that cheered me up. Until
this talk I had decided that there was absolutely nothing
good about Kathy, but her simple gesture of friendship

showed me how wrong I was. We can now talk with sincerity about travels, studies and work. Unfortunately, music is still a sensitive subject.

This experience showed me that everyone has good qualities, and we should give them a fair chance to prove it.

MY FATHER, A CONSTRUCTION WORKER

It was a perfect summer night, the Saturday before I came up to Provo to attend school. The air was warm as I walked my date to her seat and helped her remove her sweater. I had wanted to date this girl the whole summer, and now I had my chance.

The entertainment for the evening was being provided by the Mormon Choir of Southern California. The conductor, Frederick Davis, came to the front of the auditorium. He thanked the audience for giving the choir the opportunity to perform. Then he went on to say how much he enjoyed and appreciated performing in such an auditorium, with its fine acoustic qualities and beauties. It struck me then that my father was the man responsible for building that beautiful auditorium and many of the other buildings in our community. Many times when I was asked what kind of work my father did, I would shy away from the question, having the misconception that it was embarrassing for my father to be in construction work.

At the thought, tears came to my eyes, and I began to think of the mistake I had made. Needless to say, I enjoyed that concert as I have never enjoyed a concert before. I made a vow never again to be ashamed of the kind of work my father did, especially because my father was the one who was doing it.

KNOWLEDGE

SPELUNKING

One particular experience that I remember well happened when I went spelunking with one of my classes. This was my very first experience of this sort, and I felt the fear one naturally would when doing this sort of sport for the first time. We had been told that for the first fifteen feet, we would not have a safety line attached, because the chances of falling all the way to the bottom were almost impossible. (However, I have been known to do the impossible.) I enjoyed the trip down into the cave and back. The bad part started when we were just forty feet from the place where you go back up. One of the girls in my group fell or slipped, hurting her knee. The accident shook the rest of us badly. Then the time came to climb back up. I was called to go first. I was tired, sore, and scared. About half way up, I found I had no strength in my arms. How easy it would have been to just let go! I was so tired! I hurt. I didn't even care about falling anymore. When I was ready give up, the girl who had hurt her knee called up to me encouragingly and told me she needed me to help her up. I couldn't give up then, and new strength came to me.

SPICY HOT

While we were in Japan on a military tour of duty, we were invited to a Shinto wedding. After the wedding, we were also invited to attend the reception—each of us sat on cushions on the floor with a tray of traditional Japanese wedding food in front of us. I sat next to the bride's father, who spoke no English; I spoke only limited Japanese. He pointed to a tiny container of food and said, "Oishii desu," which, interpreted, means, "This is delicious." I thanked him and took a goodly portion on my hashi (chop sticks) and put it into my mouth. I thought I was going to die right on the spot! It was so hot that it burned all the way down. I had eaten something similar to horseradish, only much hotter.

A few days after the wedding, the bride and her father came to our house to visit me. As we began talking about the wedding the bride said, "My father was very surprised when you took such a big bite of the spice. It is very hot." I replied, "Well, he wasn't nearly as surprised as I was. He said it was delicious, and I took his word for it. I thought I was going to die." How they laughed. She said in reply, "Yes, it is delicious, but only in tiny amounts, and it is always eaten with other foods—never alone."

A little learning is a dangerous thing.

CHANGING A BEHAVIOR

A year ago when I was in college, my cousin invited me to live off campus with her for a term because she didn't want to live alone for two months.

Well, she and I get along exceptionally well, so I accepted, and we began our adventure of living together. One of the experiences we had was extremely interesting and fun for me.

I was taking a child psychology class at the time. One of the assignments dealt with changing a person's behavior by reinforcing whenever the desired behavior was performed.

I decided to change my cousin's behavior from being sleepy to being more awake in the mornings. My plan was to get her to say good morning to me when we were up together in the morning (she always said she was too tired to say anything in the morning). So I made a deal with her that if she would say good morning to me, I would give her a Snickers candy bar.

The first morning she forgot so she didn't get her candy bar. I reminded her that she could try again the next morning.

The second morning, she didn't say anything to me, so I looked at her with a questioning, expectant look. Then she remembered and said good morning, so I rewarded her with a Snickers candy bar. Her eyes just about popped out of her head, because she didn't really think I'd do it.

The next morning she said good morning to me twice! So she got one candy bar in the morning and one in the afternoon as her reward.

Well, as it was, saying good morning to me wasn't so hard to do when she got rewarded for it. Later on she would find that saying good morning was a nice way to start the day, whether she got a candy bar or not, because the social reinforcement would be enough reward.

The moral or the application of this experience is that how even little things can be rewarding to us and to others. We don't always have to have a material reward to feel good. It can be social and internal, too.

FINGER IN THE PULLEY

One day while working on a farm, I was driving a tractor pulling a disk plow. I was plowing out weeds about three feet high and they kept getting stuck between the disks. I stopped the tractor several times and cleaned out the weeds, but it kept getting clogged. So rather than keep on stopping the tractor, I began jumping off while it was still moving to pull the weeds out. Then I would jump on again.

One time as I was jumping back onto the tractor, my footing slipped and my hand fell on the track on one side and my finger got caught in the track. There I was walking alongside the tractor with my finger caught so tight there was no way to pull it out. I prayed and many things came to my mind. Luckily, as the track came to the front of the tractor, it opened for a split second and I was able to pull my finger out. Thankfully, all I lost was my fingernail.

This taught me a lesson to do things the proper way and to not try to take shortcuts.

BASKETBALL

One of the greatest experiences I have ever had happened when I was about sixteen years old. Our church ward had split a year or two before and now had all the girls in it and just a few boys. We discovered our problem in fielding a basketball team, and the outlook was not good. Those of us that were there decided that if we wanted a good team, we had to come up with some more guys. We resolved to pull ourselves together and get a ward list. We went down the list and found every eligible boy in the ward. It didn't matter to us whether he was short, tall, active or inactive, popular or outcast—we called everyone and asked them to come out.

At our first meeting we had such a good turnout that we decided to field two teams, one to play to win, and one to play for fun. We also made the commitment (those of us on the team to win) to practice two or three times a week no matter what the required sacrifice. We put everything we had into the team, and although there was not one person on our team that was six feet tall, somehow we won a tough stake championship. We went on to zone play-offs and won that too. The beautiful thing about it was that we activated several boys and made them a part of a pretty good organization. The friendships developed there were great! We laughed together, we played together, we practiced together, we attended church together. We also worked together to earn uniforms, we learned discipline together, and finally in the bitter end, we cried together because something we worked so hard to accomplish fell through our fingers when we were disqualified through a technicality that was not our fault.

We didn't come away empty-handed, though, because in the process we gained a victory. Not a victory over our opponents but a victory over ourselves. We learned a little about sacrifice and what it meant to be a friend; we felt the value of the church, and learned a lot about teamwork and what total effort meant to achievement. We learned about compassion and sportsmanship. Basically, we learned the important lessons of life, and we did it because we cared. In other words, we learned in a very real way what the gospel of Jesus Christ is all about.

BOO!

One day my roommate and I went jogging on the track at the Smith Fieldhouse. After we finished, she stopped to get a drink of water while I kept walking. After I turned the corner, I decided to stop and startle her when she came around the corner. I stood there and listened. Within about thirty seconds, I heard footsteps. I got ready and as the person came around the corner, I said, "boo!" Well, it wasn't my roommate. It was a young man—my roommate was behind him. Boy, was I embarrassed.

When we choose to close our eyes by not looking at what's coming our way, we may find that it isn't what we were expecting. We need to keep our eyes open so that we will be prepared for the experiences coming to us.

FINGER-GET-STUCK-MISFIT

I am a finger-get-stuck-misfit. There are not many of us around. You see, a finger-get-stuck-misfit is a person who, no matter how hard he or she tries, gets a finger stuck in anything. In fact, it doesn't even have to be a finger. It can be an arm, a foot, a head, or a whole body.

This unique talent of mine started when I was fourteen years old. I was participating at a regional gymnastics meet. I was adjusting the uneven bars when the knob I was turning slipped and caught my finger between it and the bar. After about a minute, I had enough courage to look over at the head judge, wondering how I was going to tell her. She finally worked my finger out, but not until all the judges and spectators knew what was going on.

It was after that experience that the hex was put on me. Everything I looked at got stuck somehow on my body. Bottles were and still are a morbid fear of mine. They seem to just reach out and grab my hand without warning.

I remember a time about two years ago when I went shopping with my mom. I was busily walking down the isles of the supermarket, finding things on my mother's list. I went to reach up to a shelf for something, but my hand wouldn't move. I looked down and to my dismay—there my finger was stuck to some wires of the cart. I tried for about 30 minutes to get it out, but it wouldn't budge. I decided after seeing that my finger was blue that it was time to call for help. It wasn't until the employees had picked themselves off the ground from laughing that I got my finger out. It came out easily after Vaseline, grease and a crowbar were applied.

I don't think I would mind holding this habit of mine if I wouldn't use it in public, but it seems that it's the only time it goes to work. I was visiting a friend in the hospital when the power took over again. We had been having a nice conversation when I realized it was time to go. I turned to leave, but didn't. My body was willing, but my little finger wasn't. I didn't even have to look down to see what was wrong. I knew. It was only after two nurses, one orderly and two maintenance men came that I was free. They told me they didn't mind taking the corner of the bed apart. It was good practice.

My poor mother is really the one who suffers. It's kind of hard to explain why her daughter's fingers are always black and blue. But the worst was when I was the program chair-

man at my old high school. It was between assemblies and I
was talking to some friends. We had been using the podium
that day, and through no fault of my own, I again got stuck
(stuck in a tiny hole on top of the podium). This time my
finger was released after the counselors, students, teacher,
and principal had a look (not mentioning the pictures for
the school newspaper and having to be carried with a giant
podium down the halls and out to the shop building). The
podium is still standing, but now with a massive sawed-out
hole in the top.

There is one thing I can be proud of, though. Through all
the bottles, podiums, shopping carts, and uneven bars, I've
never had a break yet.

Embarrassment plus time equals humor.

FALLING OFF PONIES

One day my brother Bud and I were riding home on our
ponies down a dirt road. My brother wanted to find out who
had the fastest pony, so he challenged me to a race home. We
both took off at full speed, and as my brother passed me, his
pony bucked him off and he fell to the ground. I stopped as
quickly as possible to see what I could do. Bud, in pain, cried
for me to go get my mother. I jumped back onto my pony
and went towards home. Well, no sooner had I started when
the saddle slipped sideways, and I fell off. Both my brother
and I lay crying in the dirt.

As we travel down the road of life, we must prepare ourselves mentally, physically, and spiritually for life's ups and
downs. If we do not prepare ourselves, we cannot be of assistance to anyone else—we have no strength for helping ourselves. If we do not help others, we are not following God's
commandment to love our neighbors. In following his teach-
ings, we will first prepare ourselves, and then we will be able
to help others.

SKIING

It was a bright but cold winter day. The ski slopes were beckoning skiers to enjoy the newly fallen powder. I had been skiing twice before and had always skied on the beginners' slopes. I knew I was going to stay on the beginners' hill again because I knew the intermediate slopes would be too hard for me.

After awhile, I could breeze down the beginners' slopes without any problems, but I was afraid to try the harder slopes. After some persuasion by my friends, however, I decided to try it.

On reaching the top of one of the intermediate slopes, panic struck me, and I could not see any possible way I could get down. But I got up some courage and found that if I went slowly, mogul by mogul, I could get down. It might take an hour, but eventually I'd get down.

The second time down was much easier.

Life's progression is so very much like my experience. Many times we're afraid to take a giant step onto something more challenging. But if we can remember that progression takes time, and that when we take something upon ourselves, we must really strive to reach it, we can attain it if we take it slowly, mogul by mogul.

SEEK AND YE SHALL FIND

I remember sitting with my best friend at a youth group meeting of the Protestant church I then belonged to. Both of us were making comments and asking questions like, "What is heaven really like?" "Surely there must be marriage after death." "What do you do in heaven?" and "Is there really a hell?"

Our conversation went on and on, but neither of us were able to answer any of the questions we asked. Finally, we posed our questions to the minister. I remember the turmoil on my friend's face as the minister answered our questions with words that meant absolutely nothing. The greatest let-down of all came when the minister said to us, "No, you don't remain married after death." My friend and I had both taken it for granted that all couples remained together after death, and the disappointment we felt as we listened to the minister's answers was great.

My questions did not cease at the end of that meeting, however. I kept asking questions and finally got the answers. Now I have been a member of The Church of Jesus Christ of Latter-day Saints for three years. My friend, unfortunately, is still looking for the answers to those questions.

Never give up. Seek and ye shall find. Knock and it shall be opened unto you.

SLEIGH RIDE

One sunny, winter day, my roommates and I went sleigh riding. On one of the trips down the hill, three of us went together on a small sleigh. But there were too many of us, so we went very slowly, stopping every few minutes. Realizing that one of us had to get off to allow the other two to continue, I jumped off. With the load lighter, and with only two bodies to balance and guide the sleigh, my roommates rode down to the bottom of the run without stopping.

The number of people on the sleigh is like the times we plan to do too much in a short time. Because we let things pile up, the whole pile becomes too much to handle. Therefore, we need to stop, analyze the situation, and redistribute our time and the issues involved. Doing this will let us accomplish our goals one step at a time until we reach the end of the hill.

THE SPIDER

I was lying on my bed, too tired to move or get ready for bed, when I heard my name faintly and timidly called,

"Jane...Jane." Finally, I rose from the mattress and went into the hall to find my roommate Eileen pointing into the bathroom.

"It's in there," she said.

I didn't understand for a moment, but then I saw the brown, long-legged meadow spider on the wall.

Very confidently, I told her to stand ready at the front door, but first to get me a piece of paper.

I thought it would be easy to catch the spider, as I held up the paper near the spider so he could crawl on. No such luck. He reared back on his back legs as I prodded him with the paper and then ran away from me down the wall. I tried again and the same thing happened. Finally, he did hop onto the paper, but he didn't stop there (as all good spiders should, I thought). Fear gripped me as the little, brown body moved speedily toward me. In less than a second, paper and spider flew into the air to land in the bathroom tub as I added some vocal support, known as a scream. I rushed out of the bathroom, and seeing Eileen's excited, questioning face, I broke into uncontrollable laughter.

We tried calling our home teachers—who weren't home. Then Eileen had a great idea. We got Linda Cluff, a zoology graduate student, to save the day with a simple invention: a jar and paper. She captured the misplaced spider and escorted him to the outdoors.

Don't be bashful in the face of frightening situations. Learn to have patience when looking for solutions to problems.

LITTLE BABY RABBITS

I grew up on a farm in Washington State. During my childhood, we had many farm animals and pets including a number of rabbits. One cold February day when I was about seven, one of our mother rabbits gave birth to six little babies. We were delighted. But when my younger brothers and I went to see the baby rabbits the next night, we found that the mother had left them and that they had frozen. Brokenhearted, we put them in front of a heater and sat and cried and prayed. When our mother got home, she found three crying lads and six warm but still dead little rabbits.. We learned that night that our Heavenly Father, just like our earthly parents, can't give us everything we want and ask for.

MISCOMMUNICATION

One evening, as I was helping my mother prepare supper, she turned to me and said, "Will you warm the rolls in the oven, please." I had never warmed the roles in the oven before, so I asked her how to do it.

"Put them in a plastic bag, then put them in the oven," she said.

"But the bag will melt," I said.

"No, it won't," she told me while busily doing a million other things.

"But mother," I argued, "it will too!"

"Not if you put water in it first," my mother answered.

I knew she was just busy and only half listening, so I decided not to argue anymore. I proceeded to put the rolls in a plastic bag. Then I ran water over the bag and placed them in the hot oven.

A few minutes later, my mother opened the oven to find a bunch of plastic-covered rolls. I got yelled at for being so stupid.

"I said a paper bag," she insisted, "not a plastic bag!"

But I knew what I had heard. In the end, we both laughed, and the experience has become a family joke whenever cooking skills are mentioned.

Communication is a must. A person needs to be able to listen as well as convey meaning in a clear manner.

TEACHING WITH AN EXPERIENCE

There was a young woman in the hospital bed next to mine who had spent the previous three months in the intensive care unit. She had her head wrapped with bandages, which were secured at the base of her neck. Her body was so frail that there hardly seemed enough skin to cover her protruding bones. She was pale and weak. She could not sit up or feed herself; she was literally helpless to see to her own physical needs.

When I asked one of the nurses about this young woman, she replied that she had had surgery to remove a brain tumor. Tears sprang to my eyes at this. I felt so guilty for all the complaining I had done. I could do so much more than she. Silently, I said a prayer which burned in my heart: "Oh, Father, what gratitude I feel for the health I have. Forgive me for thinking my lot is hard. But all is well." My heart ached for the young woman—I will never forget that feeling. "I complained because I had no shoes until I saw a man who had no feet." We need to appreciate all the blessings we have been given.

SWIMMING LESSON

It was a hot, bright summer day and we had just opened up the public swimming pool for the summer. I was sitting in the guard chair nearest the diving boards, thinking of everything and yet nothing.

Two little kids soon came over to the boards to dive. They both climbed up on to one board and so I picked up my megaphone to tell them that only one person was allowed on the boards at a time. One of the other guards had spotted the kids too and asked them if they knew how to swim. For a response, one of them climbed back down the board. I watched carefully while the bigger of the two children walked to the end of the board and jumped in.

Unfortunately, she had forgotten to tell me that she couldn't swim either. I found this out soon enough, and before I knew it I had a whistle in my mouth and was flying through the air. I swam to her and somehow got her to the side of the pool, where my manager and a few other guards were ready to help.

I learned the lesson of being prepared. For most of the summer I had sat in a chair and done nothing but watch little kids swim. It might not have seemed important, but I was there, ready and prepared just in case someone really did need me.

STICK TO IT

One of the greatest lessons I learned was taught me while hiking in the Teton Mountains. A small group of us began hiking Table Rock mountain early one morning in July. The weather was fairly warm, and there were a few clouds. But after we were about three-fourths of the way up the mountain, the rain began to fall. We put on our raingear and sat under some trees, waiting for the storm to pass.

After about twenty minutes, the rain did not stop, and we continued on with the hike, determined to make it to the top. The sun finally came out, giving us the extra encouragement we needed. Even though the sun was out, the air was still cold because of the high altitude. Pretty soon the sun disappeared and it began to snow. But this time, we were past the timberline, so we had no shelter. We were hiking on shale rock, which becomes slick when wet. The wind was blowing, which made our visibility very poor. Conditions weren't exactly ideal for hiking. However, we were determined to make it to the top, so we continued to climb—on our hands and knees. We kept climbing until we made it to the top. We had accomplished our goal.

I had mixed feelings while hiking. When it started to rain and was cold, part of me wanted to quit and go back to the car, but the other part of me wanted to continue on, just to prove that I could make it. Obstacles kept getting in the way, but I told myself that I could overcome those obstacles, and I did.

It is often possible to achieve goals we set. There will be storms and obstacles along the path, but if we want to succeed, we may be able to, no matter how difficult it is.

THE TOP OF TIMPANOGOS

Last fall my husband and I decided to climb to the top of Mt. Timpanogos. During the previous week, we had climbed to Timpanogos Cave ƒa good steep climb. My husband got the idea to go to the top and I half-heartedly agreed, although I realized that after the short hike to the caves that I was in no condition for the eighteen-mile hike that lay ahead of me.

The following Friday night, we camped at the bottom of the mountain. The next day, we woke up to a beautiful morning to begin our hike. The first two to three miles we had no problems. We were below the timber line. Lush greenery, fresh underground springs and little waterfalls were everywhere. The hiking was easy—long switchbacks on a very low incline. I was elated with the beauty around me and the fantastic view that became more and more vast the higher we climbed.

Then we began to come out of the timber. There was no water anywhere, and the surroundings were becoming less and less spectacular. The vegetation was all dry. Because I only had tennis shoes on, blisters were starting on my feet. Every step reminded me that they were getting worse. To top things off, the sky was becoming overcast.

All my senses said, "It's time to go back—you can go to the top another day," but my husband kept encouraging me to keep going. We did make it to the top, and oh, the view we were rewarded with. But better yet was the feeling I had that I hadn't given up.

I learned a lesson that day. While climbing I could see that enduring to the end of life was like climbing the mountain. First I realized how important preparedness was: our trip would have been a lot easier had we gotten physically in shape, found out how much water was on the mountain, what the climate conditions were like, and dressed accordingly. So is life also easier if we prepare for the trials that face us. It becomes important to talk to others who are older and experienced in order to gain from their wisdom and to heed the warnings and counsel. It is important, for example, to heed the counsel of the General Authorities.

Traveling through the lush green area reminded me of my youth at home. Everything was very nice—problems were minimal and easy to solve. Now, while away from home, struggling along with my husband to finish school and meet our financial needs, the solutions sometimes don't seem as obvious. By sticking to that path, we can make it back to him. How glorious will be our reward—as was my reward when I finally made it to the top of Mt. Timpanogos.

BITE FROM MAMA

One warm and sunny day, I was outside playing when I noticed that a neighbor girl was standing in front of our house, eating a Tootsie Roll. I wanted to have some, so I went to her and asked for a piece. She wouldn't give me any, so I bit her arm. She dropped the Tootsie Roll; I grabbed it and took a large bite from it. By this time, my mother had noticed what was happening. She came outside and dragged me back into the house, rolled up my sleeve, and bit my arm.

I learned from this experience that you can't always receive what you want—even if you try force, for there is punishment. (I also learned that you shouldn't bite other people.)

Keeping Your Mouth Shut

During my freshman year, my roommate and I had secret pen pals who lived in the boys' dorm. One day they informed us that our letter writing would have to come to an end because they were being kicked out of BYU for stealing over $300.00 of merchandise. Loving excitement, my roommate and I made arrangements to meet them at dinner in the Cannon Center. While standing in line waiting for food, we verbally speculated on who in the room would turn out to be our thieves. That night we received a phone call. It was our friends the thieves. They had heard everything we'd said because they'd been standing right next to us in line at the cafeteria. We were very embarrassed!

Never talk behind people's backs. It will surely get back to them.

Batteries

I used to own an old car. It ran extremely well, and I never had any problems with it. After I had owned the car for about two years, I decided to buy a new battery for it. I bought the battery and had it installed at the local garage.

About a month later, as I was driving home from a date about thirty miles away, my headlights kept getting dimmer and dimmer. I was angry, because I had just bought the battery. The next day I took my car down to the garage to complain. I was told that my battery was okay, but my generator was gone. No matter how well my battery stored electricity, it had to have a source of receiving new power.

Our testimonies are the same way. We can have the strongest testimonies in the world, but they still need to be replenished once in a while. We need to continually renew our testimonies by going to church and associating with people who share our beliefs.

Effort

I'll never forget the many hours I spent on a little Massey Ferguson tractor out on our fifty-acre farm. Our fields were irrigated, and about every two feet was a small furrow which ran down the field. While cutting hay or working on some other job, I often noted an interesting thing: Whenever the tractor wheels slipped into these small ruts, there was an extra pull felt on the engine. A little more gas was required to pull the tractor out onto smooth ground.

Quite often in life, we slip down into those little ruts and feel the extra pull. If we can exert a little more effort, we can get back on top things where the going is smooth.

Following the line of least resistance will make men, like rivers, run crooked. The only difference between a rut and a groove is the dimension.

Valentine's Day

It was Valentine's Day, and my class was to make valentines and place them in a box. I knew I would never get a valentine from anyone in the class, so I sent my valentines to myself. As the teacher drew each card from the box and read each name, my name was read:

"One, two, three," the teacher said. "My, you have a lot of friends."

But it backfired!

"I saw him make those valentines himself," the girl sitting next to me said.

I was terribly ashamed and embarrassed as the class giggled and laughed.

Many times, it isn't the mistake, but the way we try to cover it up that hurts. Always be in the open and you will be happy.

Personal Experience

When I was a little girl of ten I visited the house of my neighbor. He had boards, nails, and all kinds of things in his yard. It was like a junk yard.

Well, I had a brainy idea that I wanted to know what it felt like to step on a nail. So I picked a nail out and stepped on it. Blood started gushing out of my foot, and I started screaming. I'm not really sure if I was crying more from the pain or from the sight of all the blood. My father came to save the day, taking me to the doctor, who took care of me properly.

Learn from the experiences of others. I knew it would hurt me to step on the nail—other people had told me. Think before you act.

Be Prepared

I was stationed on a Forest Service fire Lookout on the border of the Idaho Primitive Area, a place that had to be supplied by mule train, since there was no road to the lookout.

The fire danger was low one weekend, so I got permission to walk out from the lookout for a couple of days. After my short stay in town, I headed back. I was driven to where the trail started, and then began about a six-mile walk. When I started up the trail, my watch showed that I had enough time to make it to the lookout before dark. I later found that the stem on my watch had been pulled out, and I only made it about halfway before it got dark. I stopped to get my flashlight out, but found that it didn't work. A little later I could hear a bear a short distance from me. I froze. I had not brought my rifle with me. The bear soon went away. I spent most of the night on the hill, but finally got my flashlight repaired and made it back to the lookout.

I learned three lessons from this experience: one, be prepared; two, remain calm under stress; and three, the Lord will help and watch over us.

Put on the Brakes

When I was about twelve years old I lived on a farm. Because I was one of the youngest children, I never learned how to run the farm equipment like the rest of the kids. One day my brother asked me to steer the tractor while he pulled it with the car so the tractor would start and he could get some farm work done. I told him I didn't know how to drive the tractor, but he assured me it was easy, so I consented.

He hooked the car in front and started pulling the tractor while I steered it, until the tractor started. When it started it began going on its own power. I thought that if I stepped on the brake, it would stop, but it didn't. I didn't know that I was supposed to pull out the clutch in order to stop it, so I ran the tractor into the back of the car. On the front of the trac- tor was a large, wooden saw, used to cut firewood. A metal bar stuck out about three feet in front to hold the logs up while they were being cut. I heavily damaged the car. Don't start anything unless you know how to stop it. Don't rely on someone else's experience to do something.

The Rush Ride

One summer day when I was ten years old, I was preparing to go to Girl Scout camp. The bus was to leave at a designated time; if I wasn't there it would go without me. For some reason I was late, and so was in a terrible rush to not miss the bus. My brother and his bike were my transportation to the bus stop.

We were riding double, and since he knew I was in a hurry, he took a short-cut over a bumpy road. Gaining in speed and hitting those rough spots, we crashed and fell. No major damage was done (we were still alive!), but we did have cuts and bruises, and I fractured my arm. This was enough to curtail my Girl Scout camp adventure. Instead, I spent my summer incapacitated with one arm in a sling!

"Short-cuts" don't always pay off. It's usually wiser in the long run to be cautious and do things right, even if it takes more time!

KEEPING ON THE SAFE SIDE

A group of us kids were outside playing. There was a wild cow with long horns in the pasture near us. We decided we would see who could milk her, so we approached her, trying to sneak a little closer every time without disturbing her. She just stood there watching us, giving us a speculative eye. All of a sudden, she charged at my youngest brother, Wayne, who was seven years old. We watched in horror as he lowered her horns and went after him. I've never seen anyone run so fast in my life. When he reached the fence, he simply flung himself through the barbed wires. We were very lucky no one was hurt. That day we learned that as with all matters of life, we must be careful to stay away from temptation and not try to see how close we can get before getting hurt.

THE SWING

When my family lived in Georgia, we had a great swing that hung from a giant oak tree. I remember the fun I had swinging through the air. One day, I wanted to try something new, however. As the swing was up in the air, I hooked my knees over the seat and bent over backwards until I could see where I was going. It was a great position all the way to the top and most of the way down, but underneath the swing, there wasn't enough room between it and the ground. I was dragged face down and it really messed me up. The lesson that I learned is that you should think things through before you act.

ADVICE FOR EVERYONE

I was making chocolate chip cookies recently with my four children. I had just commented to three-year-old Jill that she needed to keep her fingers away from the beaters, or they would get chopped off. Not more than thirty seconds after my admonition, I had the index finger on my left hand caught and the tip torn to the bone. I immediately wrapped the finger in a wash rag and called my husband. We went to the hospital and had the tip stitched back on. It healed, but still looks very deformed.

As I analyzed this experience, I realized that I myself was overly confident when using the Mix Master. I would use my fingers to scrape off batter as the beaters were turning slowly, not realizing just how easily my fingers could get caught. I realized that we must never be too confident. The devil will catch us if we are not on our guard. My deformed finger will constantly remind me to run from temptation, lest I be caught and possibly cause scarring to my soul.

YOU CAN DO IT!

When I decided to take up mountain climbing, my friend who was going to teach me to repel told me, "If you want to learn this skill, don't give up until you've done it at least once." I said that I would try it at least once.

I was to anchor a rope to the mountain, tie the other end of the rope around my waist, back down the steep cliff, push away from the face of the cliff, and drop twenty feet.

As I started backing off the cliff I got scared. My friend encouraged me. "Just once," he said. "It's safe. The rope is safely anchored and tied to your waist. Try it just once."

Still frightened, I remembered that when my friend offered to teach me I had promised to try it at least once. For a moment, I overcame my fears and started down the cliff. No one was more surprised than I was when I reached the ground safely. I had done it once. Now I felt the self-esteem and confidence of accomplishment. Eagerly, I ran back up the mountain to do it again.

As we overcome fear, we gain confidence and self-esteem. The next time we do something hard, we know we can do it.

CHOICE AND ACCOUNTABILITY

HAULING HAY

When I was very small, Mom and Dad had to work very hard on our farm to make a good living. One day, when they went to the field to haul hay, they told me to stay home and play with the old record player until they came home for dinner. I decided instead to go see how the work was coming along. The cool sand felt good on my bare feet, but when I walked on the hay stubble, it cut my feet. By the time I finally got to where Mom and Dad were, my feet were bleeding profusely. I couldn't walk for a week because of the soreness—all because I didn't listen to my parents.

Honor thy father and thy mother, that thy days may be long upon the land which the Lord thy God giveth thee.

EATING TACOS

When I was no more than two years old, I was sitting with my parents at our small kitchen table, eating one of our favorite dinners: tacos. I remember watching my parents garnish their tacos with lettuce, tomatoes, cheese, and Tabasco sauce. I likewise proceeded to heap my taco with lettuce, tomatoes, and cheese, but when I reached for the Tabasco sauce, my parents stopped me gently. I persisted in my efforts, but still my parents did not yield. In utter frustration, I burst into tears and, despite my mother's protests, my father uncapped the bottle of sauce and handed it to me. I sprinkled the Tabasco sauce liberally over my taco. My first big bite told me I had made a poor choice. My mouth burned, and I again cried—this time from shock and pain. I have never forgotten that experience, or the feeling that I should have followed my parents' guidance.

Listening to the counsel of those who have experience may prevent us from hurting ourselves.

MILKSHAKES

When I was four years old, I was sitting at the table getting ready to eat. I was excited because this particular night we were having milkshakes with our meal. Before we began eating, we were told to stir up our milkshakes because they had not been fully mixed. After the prayer, I lifted up my glass to my mouth without stirring my milkshake. Nothing would come, so I tilted the glass even further. Suddenly and unexpectedly, the ice cream fell upon my face, covering every inch and taking my breath away.

Unless we follow the directions of our leaders, Satan with his temptations will smother us and tempt us to do evil.

HONESTY

In my eighth grade English class, I was doing fairly well in my studies, though all the cheerleaders and football players were in my class. All we did in class was mess around and play. Our teacher got used to us, so our playing during class didn't affect her as it would have affected other teachers.

One day, she assigned us all topics to prepare for speeches. None of us wanted to prepare a speech, but she required us to. Although we had a week to prepare, we didn't prepare well enough.

None of us did exceptionally well on our speeches. After the presentations were over, our teacher passed around the roll book which included our grades. Some people changed their grades, holding the book underneath the table so the teacher couldn't see. When the book came to me, I also changed my grade, from a D+ to a B+. Later that day, my teacher called me into her room and yelled at me. Scared, I started to flatter her so she would give me a good grade in English, along with an "S" (for "satisfactory") in citizenship.

When graduation day came, all the students went to their homeroom class to get their report cards. I rushed to my class and grabbed my report card. The grade I got in English was a C+ but my citizenship grade was a "U" for unsatisfactory. That spoiled my whole day because I had never before received a "U," and here was my first on graduation day. I was so upset that I began to cry. My parents had no idea what upset me, so I had to tell them. My father told me that what I had done was cheating.

THE HOT DOG

Once, my family went out for hot dogs and then went to the park to play and have a picnic. I was small, not more than four or five years old, and I got awfully tired of my hot dog. The other kids were playing already and I was only halfway finished with my hot dog, so I slipped it under the picnic table and went off to play. Not soon after, my mom called to us to go home. We all went, tired and exhausted, to the car. We had already begun to leave when my father asked who had thrown the hot dog under the table. Of course my brothers and sisters all denied it. And so did I. My parents, however, knew I was guilty, and I was chastised and spanked. My father explained, however, that the reason I was getting spanked was because I lied to him, and not because I threw the hot dog away.

A TASTY EXPERIENCE

One night I sneaked a sandwich to bed. I had my light turned off so that my mother wouldn't know that I was awake. I dropped a piece of meat, so I felt around in the dark until I found it. As I chewed it I realized it didn't taste much like meat. I hurriedly turned on the light and saw that I had chewed a stink-bug.

When we try to deceive others, we are the one that suffers.

The Dress

When I was in high school my mother took me to town and told me to pick out the prettiest piece of wool fabric that I could find. She was going to make a new dress for my sister's birthday and surprise her. Since I wore the same dress size, my mother asked me to help pick out the material, act as the model and do a little sewing in my spare time.

Since the dress was to be for my sister, and not me, I wasn't careful to choose the best material. I just picked out something I could find in a hurry. When I sewed it, I wasn't as careful with seams and zippers as I would have been with my own dress.

We finished the dress about the first of December and we put it away for her birthday in January. I forgot about that dress until Christmas morning when I opened my packages. There it was. It had been for me all of this time.

Do unto others as you would have them do unto you. Our deeds, good or bad, will come back to us.

The Bad Play

I was the quarterback on the football team during a game two years ago when I learned a lesson. I had called a play that required me to go to my right with the football and eventually run or pass. The play was designed naturally to have the blocking set up to the side I was moving to.

When I went to the line, I was confused at first by the defense being put up against us. I noticed that one man was completely out of position on the defense, so I decided to call an audible and change the play at the line of scrimmage. I made the change using the system that our team used. However, I made a mistake in the change. I thought I had changed the play to go to the left to take advantage of the weakness of the defense in that area.

As I took the ball from the center, I went to the left while the rest of the team went to the right. I was immediately tackled for a five-yard loss.

We should always be aware of what we are thinking and doing, and always try to act in the correct way. The rewards are much greater if we behave in the right manner than if we go off on our own path and thereby face destruction.

SMOKING EXPERIMENT

When I was almost twelve years old my friend and I began experimenting with smoking. We wanted to find out what it was all about. At this time I was approaching my twelfth birthday and the calling of a Deacon in the Aaronic Priesthood. I knew I should tell my bishop, but couldn't because he was such a good friend of our family, and I thought he would think less of me.

I didn't want to tell my parents either, but something told me I should. So one night I told them in a sort of round-about way. Instead of the harsh words and spanking with a belt that I had expected, they told me how proud they were of me for telling them. They counseled me and made me feel better. When I went to see the bishop, the experience was rewarding.

Honesty really pays. I felt good inside and dedicated myself to being more honest.

BOX OF CAPS

One experience that stands out in my mind occurred when I was four years old. I remember stealing a box of caps (the kind you put in a toy gun) from a friend of mine. I was trying to convince my father by lying that I had found them on the corner. My friend came to the door and asked my dad if he knew where I was because he was missing a box of caps. Dad told him he knew where to find the caps, and he gave them to him. Dad said to me, "Go to your room." My shame was worse than any punishment.

I believe that our Heavenly Father works the same way as my father. Our punishment for breaking Heavenly Father's commandments won't be physical, but it will be mental. Our awareness of what we've done will create our reward or punishment.

SPEED DEMON

I was the kind of teenager who liked to spin tires, squeal around corners, and act like a big shot by driving fast all the time. My father, a quiet, peace-loving farmer, didn't like this behavior. But one summer he needed me to do some driving for him. All summer I drove the bailer to help him put up the hay. One day when he had to leave the field early, he gave me fair warning not to take the road through the middle of the field because there was a big ditch in it.

"Go around the edge of the field," he said. Knowing how well I liked to drive fast, he added, "And take it slow and easy."

It took longer to finish up my work than I had expected, so like a foolish child thinking that it would be faster, I drove through the middle of the field. When I came to the ditch, I almost flew out of the tractor. Crash! When I got down to see what was the matter, I found that I had broken the axle on the bailer. I was so ashamed. I never came so close to leaving home in my whole life. Our work had to wait for two weeks while we got the bailer fixed.

Those in authority over us often know best.

OUIJA BOARD PARTY

One Friday night when I was in the seventh grade all my girlfriends and I were gathered together at my friend Pam's house for a slumber party. We had enjoyed playing games and telling stories, but then Pam brought out her Ouija Board. I had never played with one of them before, so I was fascinated. We all gathered around the board and took turns asking it questions.

It was fun to begin with, but then the atmosphere of the party changed. We noticed that one particular car had passed by the house at least six times. We wondered who was in the car, so we asked the board. It started spelling out all sorts of scary things and we became extremely frightened. Some of the girls were almost crying, we were so scared.

I learned from this experience that the devil has extreme power, and he knew exactly what to do to make us afraid. I've learned not to play around with evil.

TOO YOUNG TO DIE

My best friend ReNae and I always played on the roof. My mom had told me not to play there because one of these days I might fall off. Being twelve years old and thinking I knew everything, we went there again. I went first and was going farther and farther until all of a sudden my hands started slipping. My first thoughts were to cry or to scream, but to my surprise all I could say was, "Heavenly Father, please help me! I'm too young to die! Save me!" ReNae ran to get a ladder, and made it just in time before I fell.

I learned that Mom knows best, and Heavenly Father is watching.

THE HARD TEST

I recall taking a test in a particularly hard class some time ago. I didn't understand the material and without really considering what I was doing, I looked onto my neighbor's paper and copied one of his answers. I still didn't realize the seriousness of what I had done until I had turned in my paper and walked out the door. At that time an unbearable feeling hit me, and I was filled with guilt. I would rather have failed that test instead of cheated.

Fearful of the consequences, I turned around and reentered the classroom to confess to my teacher. He was standing up front of the classroom, and every step I took seemed like a mile. I steered him into the corner and told him I had copied the answer and was ready to take the consequences. He smiled at me, put his hands on my shoulders and said, "God bless you, child." He then instructed me to mark that particular answer wrong and that there would be no more consequences. He hoped I had learned a lesson from it.

His attitude and response meant a great deal to me and the experience has left an indelible mark upon my value system. I realize the seriousness of cheating and how it can affect one's soul. I also realize the blessing of repentance and forgiveness when a wrong act is committed and sincerely regretted.

SEVENTY-FIVE MILES

Jerry and I had just finished our junior year in high school; for quite some time we had been doing things together with our parents' permission. But what our parents didn't know was that we sometimes lied about where we were going.

One night we decided to celebrate because school was out for the summer. We told our parents we were going to see a movie in another town. But instead, we passed through the town and headed for another one seventy-five miles farther away to visit some girls Jerry had told me about. As we approached the town, the road made a sharp curve. Jerry lost control of the car and it rolled twice.

We had to have our parents drive seventy miles from where they thought we would be. Jerry and I felt terrible not only because of the smashed car, but for lying to our parents and losing the trust they had in us.

You can get away with some things some of the time, but it will eventually catch up with you.

You Never Can Tell

I gave a Sunday School lesson and was very disappointed when only one girl participated. Later, that girl told me that because of the questions I had answered in that lesson, she wanted to be baptized. Sometimes your efforts have influences in places and ways you don't expect.

Stealing Candy

I still remember a certain trip to the grocery story when I was six or seven years old. While my mom was shopping, I happened to walk past the candy racks. I saw rows and rows of delicious candy. Boy, what a temptation! But I didn't dare steal that big piece of blue gum that I wanted so bad because I was afraid of getting caught. And besides, I'd heard enough in Sunday School to know that stealing candy was wrong, even though it was just a little thing. So I walked away and wandered around the inside of the store for a while. But Satan wouldn't let my mind rest. He kept me thinking about that big piece of blue gum. Finally, I cased out the area, and when all was clear, I grabbed that big piece of blue gum and stuck it in my pocket.

All the way home, I could just feel people staring at me. When I got home, I hurried and put the gum in my drawer. Every day, I would open that drawer, see that gum, and feel guilt fill me up. I don't even remember chewing that gum. But I do remember those guilty feelings, and I learned a good lesson from the experience.

It doesn't really matter if you get caught stealing something—big or little. You know you did it, it was wrong, and your Heavenly Father knows you did it. Your conscience is going to keep eating at you until you've learned to overcome those kinds of temptations.

A PERSISTENT EXAMPLE

I have a very close friend, and we have been aware of each other's comings and goings for quite some time. In these following lines, I would like to describe the importance of being a good example and being persistent. As my buddy was growing up, he lived a normal child's life. His parents helped him whenever they could; they were a fairly "close-knit" family.

When he reached high school age, he began thinking about serving a mission. His parents had never told him he should go, so he really didn't concern himself with the decision. He also finally realized that his folks hadn't been sealed in the temple, and it became a perplexing problem. Well, he started to ask them why, but he didn't get a definite answer. He also interested his brother and sisters in the problem.

My friend went to college at BYU. When he returned home, no change had come about. Now after he had been exposed to so many good spirits and examples at BYU, he felt even more the desire to help his folks. He served a mission, and while he was gone, his father accepted a calling in the ward and later baptized his son. This made my friend happy.

Now my good friend is planning to be married. His parents have talked to their bishop and are planning to be sealed soon so they can join their family together and attend the oldest son's wedding.

A process of years but the progress in notable.

BEING AN EXAMPLE

Sometimes, after being exposed to negative conditions and persons of low character, some people are not able to maintain their standards. The military is often a place where this can easily happen. Recently, I attended ROTC Advanced Summer Camp at Ft. Lewis, Washington. As usual, Brigham Young University had the largest number of cadets attending the camp. Being the first female cadet from BYU to attend the camp, I was quite a novelty. It seemed as if eyes were always on us because of our large number of cadets and the fact that many knew little or nothing about us Mormons.

We had been warned about the "Returned Missionary Syndrome" or trying to convert others at camp by being too pushy, and the "Holier Than Thou Syndrome" or not associating with those who were not of our religion. In the past, some BYU cadets had fallen prey to these syndromes, thus resulting in negative feelings at the camp. Instead our emphasis was to be placed on living our religion rather than preaching it. The dozen or so of us Mormons in my platoon did a good job at doing just that. After three weeks, one non-member girl from our platoon asked, "What makes you Mormons tick? You know, I haven't met a bad Mormon yet. You can't say that about people in other religions." She had many questions about the Church and was so impressed that she asked me for a Book of Mormon.

We Need to Obey the Signs

When I was in my first semester at BYU, I had an experience that taught me about the need for obedience. My sister and I were returning to Provo, Utah, after spending the Christmas holidays in Oregon with our family. It had been a very wet and chilly Christmas in Oregon. Several storm fronts had come in, and traveler's advisories were out that the roads were quite slippery with much black ice in the mountains.

When we reached Reno, Nevada, the freeway was as smooth as a mirror. Ice, three inches thick, had become glazed on the pavement. Cars were crawling in both directions. Since we had to go so slow, we were two hours behind schedule. I was driving into the outskirts of the town at a faster pace than we'd been traveling on the freeway.

A sign warned, "Bridge ahead, slippery when wet or icy." Posted beneath the sign was the suggested speed limit, twenty miles per hour. I glanced at the speedometer, which read thirty, and I started to slow the car. Then I saw a car stalled on the bridge. In a flash, I realized I would collide with it unless I brought my car to an abrupt stop. I foolishly stomped on the brake pedal. The wheels locked and we went into a skid.

I was powerless to correct the car. We slipped off the pavement and down an embankment. We sustained no damage, and the car was fine, but we had run into a mailbox, and had completely sheared the post off at ground level. Had we reduced our speed when we first saw the warning sign, we would have had time to stop by pumping on the brakes instead of stomping on them. I think that traffic signs are just one form of warning that we need to obey. Warnings are placed to alert people of difficulty ahead; if we heed the warnings, whether on the freeway or on the road of life, we can avoid unpleasant misfortunes.

Mud Pies

When I was five years old, my sister and I loved to make mud pies. To carry the water we needed, we always used glass jars. However, my mom discovered this and told us not to use glass jars because we could hurt ourselves. Well, I loved to make mud pies so much that I wouldn't listen to my mother. I sneaked a glass jar anyway and ran to the playground's drinking fountain for the water so that my mom wouldn't find out. As I was running back to make my mud pies, I tripped and fell with my hand among the pieces of broken glass. One piece went into my hand so deeply that doctors had to operate, and since then I've had a scar on my left palm to remind my of the experience. I have learned from this experience that "mothers know best," that I should "honor my father and mother," and that "mischief gives you nothing but trouble."

Conversion

While living in Montgomery, Alabama, several years ago, I became friends with a group of girls who liked to attend the churches of others in the group. When it was my turn for the girls to come to church with me, they asked me what religion I was. I told them I was a Mormon. One of the girls came with me, and her whole family became interested. A total of nine people were baptized through this experience. I learned that it is important to remain true to your beliefs and to be a good example to those around you.

Listening to Parents' Advice

My parents had always cautioned me to not play with fire. When I was about five years old, I decided to find out why not. A neighbor friend and I put together a little pile of wood and proceeded to light it with a match. We finally got it going and I was so excited that I bent down to look closer. To my horror, I got too close and my pant leg caught on fire. I tried to slap it out, but it just kept spreading. Soon, all of my clothing was burning. My friend, who was older and apparently more experienced than I, told me to lie down and roll. I did, and soon the fire was out. I learned my lesson the hard way.

RESPECT

During my senior year in high school, I worked as a cashier in a local supermarket. Often, the conversations in the breakroom weren't of the most wholesome nature. Although none of the people I worked with knew that I was a Mormon, but I guess they noticed something different about me. When I would walk into the room, they would stop their swearing and clean up their conversations. It was exciting that they tried to understand and respect the ideals they saw in me, even though they did not know that I was a Mormon.

DRESS CODE

When I was in the tenth grade, our school went into uproar over our school dress code. Some of the girls had been wearing short skirts and sloppy, worn-out jeans. Their conduct was also far from lady-like. So, the principal decided to strictly enforce the dress code, which called for modest dress—nice pant outfits and no Levis, especially not frayed jeans.

Many of the kids rebelled because of this move. Some, though, felt that the dress code should be enforced, but we hadn't said anything. One day, I spoke up and said that I supported the dress code. Others soon joined in, and the question was finally settled. The dress code was upheld. From then on school ran smoothly, and students were better behaved.

A Lesson in Disobedience

When I was a very small girl—about three or four—my parents went away for the evening while my older sister, Michelle, and my older brother, Steven, were in charge. We were all given different responsibilities to complete before my parents got back. Soon we all got involved in a game called "Keep Out of the House." The object of the game was to lock everyone we could out of the house before they had a chance to enter. My sister Michelle, younger brother, David, and I were in the house in the act of keeping all the others out when I spied my sister Katherine running for our glass door. I threw my hand forward in an effort to keep her from coming in and felt glass cut my arm and heard the sound of crashing glass. With our responsibilities unfinished and me with my arm bleeding badly, we all nervously awaited the homecoming of my mom and dad.

If we want to be disobedient, we must pay the price, whether in this life, or in the life to come.

Living Our Best

My two brothers, Ronald and Lyle, were out in our fields rabbit hunting. They had promised my dad that they would milk the cows when they got home. Around five in the evening, it began to rain. It was one of those typical lightning and thunder storms of Southern Utah. The two boys ran to the truck and waited out the storm, then agreed that they should return home to get the milking done.

When they got home, Lyle went out to the cow pasture and began to milk his cow. Ronald was a bit slower getting to the task because he had to tie his cow to the barbed wire fence with a chain. Suddenly, from out of nowhere, a bolt of lightning struck down close to the two boys. Lyle, who had finished first, had been crossing the field with his warm bucket of milk when electricity leaped from the ground to his bucket*f*sending a jolt through his body. At the same instant, Ronald was knocked off the stool, the bucket tipped over and spilled his milk, and the cow dropped to the ground as if it were dead.

A terrified Lyle ran over to Ronald and helped him to his feet. They looked at the presumed dead body of the cow and wondered what they were going to tell dad. After a few minutes, the cow began to move and finally struggled to her feet. When the two boys entered the house, their faces were pale, they were shaking, and then they began to cry. But they managed to relate their story.

My mom asked Ronald if he had been scared that the lightning could have killed him.   He thought for a few minutes and said, "No, I wasn't. All my life I have lived as good as I knew how. If I had been killed, I wasn't afraid to go." I realized that we should all live our lives righteously so that we can tell our Father in Heaven, "I have lived as good as I could."

SHOPLIFTING

As a twelve-year-old kid, I was very enthusiastic about model airplanes. I enjoyed building them, flying them, and repairing them. As a part of this enthusiasm, I needed parts and fuel to keep the models flying. Many times I didn't have the money to buy the parts or supplies I needed, so I shoplifted them.

This occurred for a period of months, until one day the store manager of the department store where I had taken the parts called me over. We went down into the basement and had a good talk. He said he had been a policeman, and that he would turn me in to be prosecuted. He would not do that if I would return all the things I had shoplifted—worn-out or not—and then pay for them. I didn't have anything with me that I had stolen at the time, and he was happy with that fact.

I also had to tell my parents—the hardest thing of all for me to do. My parents were very wise in that they had talked to me sincerely about the fact that it is not good to want or take things that one cannot have honestly or properly. I did return all the stolen merchandise and paid for it with lots of hard work around the house.

I'll never forget this experience. I have tried my best ever since not to steal even little things. I know it is not good to take that which is not yours.

SPANISH TEST

One Friday morning when I was younger, we were having a test in a Spanish class. I took the test, but about ten minutes before class was over I noticed that I had forgotten to do a section of it. I started rushing through it but got stuck on a couple of questions. I turned my head and saw the answers on another girl's paper. In that pressure situation, I wrote down the answers and turned in my test.

Later I felt really awful, but I had to wait until Monday to do anything about it. I decided that I would tell my teacher about my mistake. Monday came and I went to class. I waited until class was over to talk with him. After I talked with him, he told me that he respected me for coming to him. Although he had seen a lot of cheating going on in our class, he never said anything. I was the only one to come in and tell him. When I left I felt very good! I learned that self-respect is more important than a good grade on my test.

OBEYING ORDERS DURING THE WAR

A Special Forces operational sergeant in Vietnam had been in the country for quite some time and knew perfectly his job and the territory in which he worked. One afternoon just before the sergeant was about to leave on his evening patrol, a young second lieutenant came up to him and said, "Sarge, there has been a change in tonight's operation: Instead of approaching the objective by route A, we want you to use route B instead. I don't have time to explain any more than that. I'll see you tomorrow afternoon."

Well, the sergeant thought about what the young second "louie" had told him and said to himself, "What does he know? He's only been here six months." Route B was not only longer, but it offered less cover and protection from ambushes by the enemy. So the sergeant decided to stick with the faster and apparently safer route A. The sergeant's patrol hadn't gone more than five hours before they were hit by a company-size unit. In this hit, five men were killed, two men wounded, and two captured.

If the sergeant had obeyed the lieutenant as he should have, he and his men would have been spared. Sometimes even with all our knowledge, we still can't see the overall plan as our Heavenly Father can. It is wise to obey his good counsel.

A FRACAS IN MEXICO

When I was in the military I ran around with the wrong crowd; it was my first time away from home, and I wanted to find out what the real world and it's people were like.

My buddies and I used to go down to Mexico for a whole weekend and shop. At night we used to go drinking and running around town. It was on one of these trips that something happened I will never forget as long as I live. We were in a cantina, or bar, and it was about 11:30 p. m. We were all pretty drunk, and one of us was with a girl who worked there. One of the natives came over and started to make passes at the girl. Well, my friend went over and hit the guy right in the mouth. The poor guy flew across the room, hit the wall and fell to the floor. Then he jumped up and ran.

At closing time, all six of us walked out of the place to find ourselves surrounded by angry Mexicans! I thought my days were over. I was never so happy to see the police in my life! By the time they came we were a bunch of hurting guys. They took us straight to jail.

We spent two weeks in that jail before the American authorities came and took us back to the base. I thought I would never get out of there. Our commanding officer said this type of thing happened about three times a year. For punishment he demoted all of us to the next lower grade and wrote "nonconformist" on our records, which held me back from getting promoted all four years. However, I did get an honorable discharge when my time was up.

Stay away from evil, and keep the Word of Wisdom.

BAD JOKE

When I was little, in about the third or fourth grade, My cousin told me a "bad" joke. The words fit into an old, well-known melody. This wasn't the kind of joke that you would want your mother to read, so I wrote it down and hid it in my room under the base of my lamp.

One day I wanted one of my friends to read it (it was too long for me to remember). I pulled it out from under the lamp, and took it down to her house. When I came home, I made the mistake of leaving it on a chair in the living room. My mother found it and read it. She made me call and apologize to all of my friends who I had let read it. I was humiliated, and I knew that I would never do anything like that again.

The Toy Block

One day when I was about six years old, I was walking down an alley near my home. I reached the home of a friend and climbed the fence to see if she was in the backyard. No one was in sight; however, my eye caught sight of a little plastic block lying in the corner of the garden. I longed to have that block. I rationalized, as I looked at it, that nobody wanted it; after all, it had just been left lying there! And besides, my friend wouldn't miss this one.

I climbed back down from the fence, walked to the back gate, carefully opened it, and slipped into the back yard. I turned my head to the right and to the left, checking the yard to make sure no one was around. Then I seized the little toy, stuffed it in the pocket of my shorts, and ran back down the alley to my home.

The longer I kept that little block, the quieter I felt. I only took it out of my pocket once in a while when I was sure nobody was around. But it wasn't fun to play with anymore. I began to wish I hadn't taken it. One day, my mother noticed me playing with it. She asked where I had gotten the block. I told her that I had found it on the way home from school. She looked straight into my eyes and asked me if I was sure. I said yes. Somehow, I knew that she knew I was lying, though she didn't say anything more about it.

I remembered what my parents and Sunday school teachers had taught me about stealing: that it was wrong—even if what you took were only something small. So I decided to take the block back. It took a lot of courage for me to decide to do it, but once I made up my mind, I was able to. I quickly ran down the alley and flung the little block over the fence. Then I ran home, crying, and told the whole story to my mother. She comforted me, told me how much she loved me, and told me of the importance of honesty in all things.

That night, before I went to bed, I prayed to my Heavenly Father and told him I was sorry. I felt much better that I had the load off my mind. That experience taught me a great lesson. I've remembered it and can discern between honest and dishonest actions. Sometimes I might slip, but I've always resolved it and repented because I truly learned the importance of honesty*f*even in small things.

LOST MARE

One month during the summer, I had the responsibility of caring for a young mare we had on our farm. She broke loose one day and wandered off. But I knew where she had gone, so I didn't hurry and try to find her. Several days went by, and finally I decided that I'd better go and get her. I found her where I though she would be, but she had entangled her rope in a fence. She had been unable to reach water for several days. She was very weak and sick, and my family was extremely angry and upset with my lack of responsibility. It took several weeks for the poor mare to recover. Often we hurt more than just ourselves.

RUNNING TO THE WRONG BASE

A couple of summers ago, my softball team had a doubleheader. When we arrived at the park to play, though, we found that the other team had forfeited our first game. We then had an hour to wait before our next. Since it was the afternoon of a summer day, and we were hot and groggy, several of us lay down in the shade of a two-foot tall tree, the only tree around, and soon fell asleep.

The next thing I knew, I was being poked in the stomach with a bat; it was my turn up. Still half asleep, I managed to bat well enough to get myself on first base. The other team over-threw the ball, though, and my team started yelling at me to go to second. I took off, ran right over the pitcher's mound, and straight to third; and of course I got out. (This is even more humorous when you realize that the position I played when my team was in the field was second base.) Stay awake and alert. Read the scriptures and Satan won't fool you.

CAR KEYS

My father's example has taught me a great deal about how to have fun with the family and to control my temper. Dad would come home tired each day from working on the farm, but he'd always take time to play a thirty-minute baseball game with me. Plus, twice each week he'd drive me into town so that I could play on my baseball team, even though it was a long and tiresome drive.

My father hardly ever lost his temper with us children. One day he ran out of gas about ten miles from town. He was trying to get home quickly, in time to his favorite golf tournament on TV. He went to a nearby farmhouse and called me to come get him and bring some extra gas. After I had arrived and filled up the truck, I decided to drive the truck home so that he could drive the car. I hopped in and took off. When I got home, I finished watching the golf tournament, wondering why Dad never arrived. After it ended, when I jumped up from the couch, I heard a jingle in my pocket—Dad's car keys. I hurried out to where he was waiting, worrying about what he might say. When I found him, he calmly asked me, "How was the tournament?" Then he just got into the car and drove home. Nothing more was ever said.

BROKEN EGGS

When I was very young, I lived near my grandparents. One day I was over their house playing with my aunt, who was my same age, when we discovered a BIG box of eggs. My grandparents own a ranch, and they used to buy eggs by the case (twelve dozen). My aunt and I commenced to break these eggs. When we had smashed eleven dozen on the floor, it got too slick for us to stand up. We didn't like swimming in broken eggs, though, and we began to cry.

It was even worse when we were caught. I learned that we shouldn't let our problems become too big, or we will be unable to stand.

GOOD WORKS

CAMPING

I once went to "Girls' Camp" with a group of certified campers from the Provo East Stake. We stayed at Arches National Monument, where many others were camping. We were the minority because we were members of The Church of Jesus Christ of Latter-day Saints. One woman approached me and asked if I was a Mormon. She said that there was a spirit of unity about our group.

We all climbed a huge rock in order to sing together, accompanied by a guitar. It was very dark when we finished, and we had attracted many listeners. Someone had a huge spotlight, which was shined on us as we climbed down from the rock. When we reached the bottom, we sang "I Am a Child of God."

This experience strengthened my testimony because we were an example to those around us. We touched many hearts and were able to give away many copies of the Book of Mormon.

A DAY AT THE BEACH

One day, a seven-year-old boy named Michael and I went to an amusement park with many rides, where we had fun. Michael seemed to be experiencing things that he hadn't before. After the amusement park, we headed for the beach, where we stayed for a few hours and had more fun. We splashed around and played games. Happiness radiated from his face.

As the tide started coming in and night began to fall, we decided to go home to get something to eat. As we started up the small hill to the restroom to change from our swim suits into our regular clothes, Michael turned to me and said, "You know somethin'—this is the funnest day I ever had in my whole life!" Then he went to change his clothes.

I was left standing there, my heart filled with joy, and my eyes filled with tears, so great was my joy and so powerful was this small boy's simple statement. Love and appreciation filled my heart for that boy's statement and for my Heavenly Father, for I knew that this was truly a blessing from his hand.

Days have passed since that wonderful, heart-touching experience, and many times the memory of those words spoken by that little seven-year-old boy and the way I felt comes back to me, giving me strength, self-confidence, and purpose in life, especially when I am alone. I don't believe I will ever forget that time in my life when I thought I was nothing and realized that in the eyes of a little boy, I was everything.

It isn't what we receive but what we give that makes life worth living.

SECOND CHANCE

If I die this very minute, it could be said of me, "You have fought a good fight; you have kept the faith." I remember the prophet Joseph Smith only lived to the age of 38 years. Yet in those very short years from 15 years to 38 years of age, Joseph Smith did more for his fellowmen save Jesus Christ.

As I lay with an open lip and bleeding profusely, and consequently in a state of shock, in an apple orchard near Shelan, Washington, this thought came to my mind. If I die, what good can be said of me? What good could they say I had done for my fellowmen in my short life of 24 years? As I lay there, off in the distance I could here the ambulance and my eyes were going glassy, and I could see things I had done in my life march in a row before me. I remembered the fights I had with my little brothers and sisters, and I remembered the times I had gotten mad at my mom and dad because of something they told me to do. I remembered the time I got upset at my teacher because of the homework assignments she had given me. And I could remember the days when I was in the mission field and I was lazy and did not want to go out and do my missionary work. And I also remembered turning down my dad's advice.

And then I remembered a highway patrolman saying, "We'd better take this one in too. He's in severe shock." And as I was picked up and placed on the liter, it seemed I could see my whole life up to that point in review. It seemed to me at the time that all you could say about me was that I had done very little for my fellowmen. And as I was taken off the litter and put on the surgery table at the hospital and the surgeon stopped the bleeding and cleaned my wound, I realized that I would live and that the Lord would give me a second chance to serve my fellowmen—that he was giving me a second chance to prepare to meet him.

Today is the day to prepare to meet God, not tomorrow or the day after tomorrow—but right now. Also, if I should die right now maybe not all good could be said about me, but at least some good could be told about me. When you are in the service of your fellowmen, you are only in the service of your God.

THE EXTRA-COLD NIGHT

When I was a young boy, my father taught me to help other people that need help. I lived on a farm in Canada, and the winters would get mighty cold. Our house was situated near the highway that was often pretty slick. As people drove down the highway it was not uncommon for them to go off the road, and we would have to pull them out.

Late one extra cold night, some friends knocked on the door. They had slid off the road and were really stuck in a huge snowdrift in the ditch. I got our tractor out of the shed, and after quite a struggle, finally pulled them out.

Since then these friends have been even greater friends. They are always doing what they can for us just because of that one very cold night a long time ago.

I learned it is best to forget what we do for others, but remember what they do for us.

A SLED AND A CAR

Our driveway was covered with snow and the street was frozen over. My roommates and I were sliding down the driveway into the street on sleds we had made out of some old paneling. It was late—around midnight.

During my last ride of the night, as I raced out into the street, I looked up and saw headlights approaching me. I jumped to my feet and began to scramble out of the way. In a desperate attempt, I dove, but to no avail. The car struck me in the hip and threw me a few feet down the road. My roommates said I was in shock, because I jumped right up and began shouting, "I'm all right!" over and over.

We went into the house, and my leg started to stiffen up. I put some ice on it and asked my roommates to give me a blessing. The next day I couldn't walk, so I rested most of the day. Toward evening, my leg began to loosen up and I could walk again. Day by day I progressively got better. Saturday came, and all that remained was a bruise.

There is power in the priesthood. Christ's promise that the faithful will be healed is true. The prayer and the experience drew me and my roommates closer together.

THE SHOE-SHINE

Upon entering the mission home in Salt Lake City, I was assigned a companion for that week named Max Brimhall from Kaysville, Utah. Max had just finished his basic training in the Marine Reserve program. He was a couple of inches shorter than I, but he was solidly built.

In one of the many meetings with the General Authorities and other leaders of the Church, the idea of getting closer to our companion in the mission field was brought out. It was suggested that we do something for somebody other than ourselves, such as polishing your companion's shoes when he didn't know it. I was pretty self-centered at this time of my life, so this little suggestion went in one ear and out the other.

The next morning I came back from showering and was getting dressed, and as I started to put on my shoes I noticed that they had quite a new shine on them. I later found out that Max had shined my shoes. That made quite an impression on me. This tough Marine-type fellow had done something for me. This was the beginning of getting away from myself, and it helped me a great deal in getting closer to my companions in the mission field. It helped me to see the wisdom in this little saying: "A person wrapped up in himself makes a pretty small bundle."

Small deeds are often the most impressive.

SERVICE EVERY DAY

One of the most important principles in the Church is that of service—being able to give to others your love and concern. When I was at Ricks I was in a service group called the "Volkyries" that helped me to change my life. I was very busy that semester, but participated in their three to four service projects a week. After this effort, I found myself to be a much kinder person to those around me. I also found that as I served others (and my Heavenly Father in a sense), I was still able to get all my school work done and maintain good grades. This was a testimony to me of how important this small principle of service was. I saw that while I was so busy and sacrificing for others, I was still able to keep up. True is the saying that it's the little things that are most important and that out of small things come great things.

This experience taught me a lesson that I wish everyone knew. Now that I am at BYU and have been for the last three years, it has been very hard finding some type of service to do everyday. However, I still practice the principle because this is really how I found myself and learned that you can't really find yourself if you don't help others.

POSITIVE EXAMPLES

Growing up in a suburb of a big city doesn't afford a child too much opportunity to see nature in green mountain pastures. So when Joyce Woolf invited me to go to her summer camp, I eagerly accepted and anticipated. What I didn't know was that this was an LDS camp. My mother made me take my sister who was a "tag-along," but this time I didn't mind, probably because I knew they'd put her in a different camp site. My sister and I never really experienced a "constant teamwork and caring for each other atmosphere." So we knew that we would gain a lot from this experience.

When we finally arrived I was very disappointed. I expected to see cabins with plumbing, a nice river close to a beautiful lodge, grassy meadows and wild flowers. Instead it was hot, dry and dusty. There were rocks, dirt, dried up weeds, no cabins, and latrines that smelled terrible. Was this Camp Liahona that everyone had been so eager to visit and enjoy? I felt like crying. Soon after my shock eased a sweet LDS girl named Baunee Ann offered to help me with my bed roll and suitcase. This was fine with me as long as she didn't expect me to help her. I then realized something that was so strange. The women weren't bossing us around. They just pitched right in and were one of the girls. Wow! I had never seen that before from adults.   All these mothers were friends with all the girls—even me.

And so in a matter of a few days by their example and by the Holy Ghost, I was converted to this church, The Church of Jesus Christ of Latter-Day Saints.

FROM SELFISH TO SELF-LESS

Some years ago there was a young woman in a recreation class. She was very unhappy and off to herself. She hadn't meant to be in the class but had registered late and had no choice.   At first she hated the class because she was shy and didn't have many friends. But Brother Heaton wouldn't stand for anyone unhappy in his classes. So he went to work, and before long had the girl enjoying herself. She learned that people want to be friends and that she was really worth something.

The girl changed her major to recreation soon after and then graduated. Yet the girl that graduated was an entirely different girl than the one who entered in the class four years before.   She was poised and confident, consious of other people rather than herself.

She couldn't make up her mind what she wanted to do afterwards. Then one year her little sister had a birthday party, and she was to entertain the young guests. She decided to be a clown and apply the fun things she had learned in her recreation classes. The party was a terrific success. Everyone enjoyed themselves and her ideas. The word spread quickly and before long she had many offers to entertain at all kinds of parties. The girl had more offers than she could possibly handle because she made people have a good time in spite of their daily problems.

At one of these parties she met a young man, and over a period of time they fell in love and married. Now she has a family of her own and is busy making her own family happy.

But she still goes around to hospitals and other places to entertain people and share happiness. Everyone who ever sees and hears her loves her. And the girl has learned that making other people happy is a very important thing.

This girl at first was self-centered—always worrying about herself. But then she learned that in order to be happy, she would have to think about others; making others happy makes us happy at the same time.

ENTERTAINING AT HOSPITALS

I used to be a solo performer in the U.S.O., where I sang mostly old love songs. Several times I went to Fitzsimmons Army Hospital and sang in some of the wards after the war. On one particular occasion, I went to the amputee ward in the hospital where there were big, good-looking men missing arms and legs. I held back my tears trying to do the best performance I possibly could. After my performance there was complete silence—no one stirred. I was hurt at first because no one applauded. But then I received the best applause ever imaginable—nearly all of the boys were in tears—they were tears of appreciation. They were too sick to do the physical activity of clapping so instead showed their gratitude in a special way. They were all just as capable of touching a person as ever!

LUCKY VOLUNTEER

In a small town tucked away in northern Atlanta, there is a mental hospital with about 800 patients. For one brief, beautiful summer it was my privilege to become a volunteer at this hospital as a friend for the patients. I was allowed complete freedom to travel the corridors and wards at will within good judgement.

The other volunteers and I were given the task of therapeutically socializing the patients. This meant being their confidantes and friends. We went to their parties, we walked together around the grounds and helped to organize and initiate programs whenever possible.

When I arrived there, fear and uncertainty were uppermost in my mind. What was I getting into? Were the patients dangerous? What if I lost my master key to the wards? How was I to initiate any programs? I was scared stiff!

I soon learned how beautiful the patients were. They loved any attention and sincere interest given to them. It never ceased to amaze me how comparatively normal the patients were except for a slight flaw that society did not approve. You couldn't help but to love these people. I learned that these patients were children of God who somehow had not managed to function well in society. These "insane" human beings have a divine spark and taught me in that one summer that we are all our Father's children and have something valuable to give.

HELPING OTHERS

I used to have two horses when I was in junior high and high school that always stood close together, with their heads facing in opposite directions. When a fly would land somewhere on one of the horses that he couldn't reach, the other horse would reach over and brush the fly off. Or if one of the horses itched, the other horse would help him scratch the spot. In the winter, the horses kept warm by standing together this way.

We all have strengths and weaknesses. Sometimes there is something that one person can't quite do, and another person can help him or her do it easily. If we can remain sensitive to the needs of others and look for ways to help them, we can make the world a more pleasant place.